Sport Flying

BY THE EDITORS OF

Flying MAGAZINE

Sport Flying

CHARLES SCRIBNER'S SONS / NEW YORK

Library of Congress Cataloging in Publication Data
Main entry under title:
Sport Flying

  Includes index.
  1. Aeronautical sports. I. Flying.
GV755.S53   797.5   75–38672
ISBN 0–684–14494–8

Portions of this book were published earlier in
Flying and in *Air Racing and Aerobatics*.

1 3 5 7 9 11 13 15 17 19 c/c 20 18 16 14 12 10 8 6 4 2

PRINTED IN THE UNITED STATES OF AMERICA

Contents

PREFACE   *vii*

INTRODUCTION: *The Fun of It*   *ix*

SECTION ONE / *Daring*

    Introduction   3

    1. AEROBATICS   6

    2. SHOWMAN   37

    3. FREE FALL   49

SECTION TWO / *Speed*

    Introduction   63

    4. AIR RACING   67

    5. THE MAKING OF CONQUEST I   86

SECTION THREE / *Escape*

    Introduction   101

    6. HANG GLIDING   103

    7. SOARING   113

    8. COMPETITIVE SOARING   125

    9. BALLOONING   146

CONTENTS

SECTION FOUR / *Craft*

    Introduction   163

    10. BUILDING IT ONESELF   166

    11. *MELMOTH*   172

SECTION FIVE / *Nostalgia*

    Introduction   187

    12. THE VENERABLES   191

    13. WARBIRDS   210

    CONCLUSION: *Something Well Worth Having*   229

    APPENDIX: *Pilot Licensing*   233

    PHOTO CREDITS   239

    INDEX   241

Preface

Of all the many uses we have created for machines that fly—long-distance travel, facilitating business transactions, waging wars, fighting fires, herding cattle, and so on and so on—none provides the degree of personal gratification that comes with flying for pure sport. Even we of the staff of *Flying* Magazine, for whom being airborne is as natural as driving a car, find in sport flying a special enjoyment and opportunity for individual expression. We love to soar in motorless aircraft, to flip ourselves upside down doing aerobatics, to stare at and even to build venerable and exotic planes, and to meet other people who also like to do these things. So this book is for us a labor of love. Converted long ago to the delights of sport flying, we hope here to make other converts among current pilots and pilots-to-be.

Sometimes we can describe such flying from a relatively detached point of view, but there are also times when only a first-person narrative can convey the intensity of the experience. There is an intimacy of sensation in free fall, for instance, that no detachment could convey. And there is in an early morning balloon flight a sense of peace that is both unforgettable and almost indescribable. Accordingly, we have, quite anonymously, reproduced some of those experiences in these pages. Anonymously, because such descriptions really amount to an amalgam of shared feelings and impressions about sport flying. In this case, names are unimportant; the experience itself is paramount.

Among the writers represented here are Norbert Aubuchon, Gordon Baxter, Peter Garrison, James Gilbert, George C. Larson, Richard B. Weeghman, Ann Welch, and Stephan Wilkinson. Anna Babij was highly instrumental in the preparation of the book. The executive editor of the project was Norbert Slepyan.

The editors of this book at Scribners have been Barbara Plumb and Laurie Graham, to whom we are grateful and who we hope will be our first converts.

ROBERT B. PARKE
Editor and Publisher, *Flying* Magazine

INTRODUCTION: *The Fun of It*

Flight means different things to different people; it is a kind of Rorschach blot into which we project our fantasies. What is flight, really?

The differences between flight in an aircraft and a ride on a funicular railway or a Ferris wheel are matters of detail, since the fundamental sensations are the same. In fact, simple flight from here to there, high in the sky, produces, as every airline passenger knows, few unusual sensations. The excitement is in the skull. Being way up there is one of those amazing facts which, like the distance to the sun or the size of an atom, must be grasped intellectually to be appreciated fully.

The myth of flight permeates our religions, our languages, our legends. Only rarely do we stop to feel ourselves in bondage to gravity, but so we are. Ease of locomotion is one of the perquisites of godhood in many religions; and in religious imagination, ancient and modern, the wings of griffins, man-headed lions, and angels have symbolized our sense that nothing is more natural than weight, and nothing more supernatural than flight. Acrobats, trapeze artists, fakirs, and high jumpers fascinate us because they seem able to undo gravity. The most super thing about Superman was that he could make a very human jump and continue it into a voyage of a thousand miles, riding on a will which we all longed to share.

So we do not have to try very hard to recognize the mystery and fascination of flight; the results of its attraction infuse our language and our art. Today, flight is an everyday reality; it influences our lives. Yet most people have never flown, and many are determined that they never will. Some have flown and never will again. For some people, the view from the cockpit through empty air to the distant, dangerous ground inspires only terror, because they always have the mind's eye fixed on the chinks in the airplane's armor. Others, believing implicitly in the soundness of the system, find in the height and isolation an intoxicating victory over the mundane. For people who love it, flight makes an offer of freedom they can't refuse, however illusory it may be. The view from an airplane is not different from the view from the top of a mountain; but what sets the flier worlds apart from the climber is the fact that he is supported by and enclosed within a capsule of such small proportions that he can identify it with himself. He feels that *he* is flying.

If few people—perhaps only a tenth of the population of the United States, and a much smaller fraction of the population of the world—have flown at all, still fewer have been in a position to be not a passenger but a pilot; and of these, fewer still have gone on to become airplane sportsmen and hobbyists. This book is about this last group, people for whom flight is the ultimate expression of their personalities. Their pursuits range from the painfully slow constructions of the amateur builders and designers of airplanes through the short hops of hang glider fliers, to the compressed and saturated accelerations of the skydiver or the racer. Flying means different things to all of them—speed, daring, escape, craft, nostalgia—but it always fulfills the sirens' promise of relief from ennui and habit. This is the world of sport flying, which sets us where the wildest dreamers of the past longed to be—and all for the sheer fun of it.

SECTION ONE *Daring*

Introduction

IN the beginning, any human flight seemed a daring thing to attempt—and indeed it was. Frail machines, inadequately understood techniques, poorly forecast weather, and the fact that pioneering always takes a toll of life and limb made aviation something only for the stout of heart. Today, small children are carried to regions of the sky where once only heroes flew. Today, more than 700,000 Americans, of whom only a relative few are airline or military pilots, have active licenses to fly aircraft. Whether one is a passenger or a pilot, as long as safety procedures are followed, travel through the air is largely routine.

Is there no daring left to flight? Unless one becomes an astronaut or a combat pilot, must one say good-bye forever to the thought of becoming a hero of the skies? No. There is plenty of opportunity left in aviation for those who like their flying served up with heart in mouth and sweat on palms, for those who want to test themselves or their ships further than most people would even want to daydream about. While it is no longer daring merely to commit oneself to flight, it is still daring to place oneself in a position from which only his own skill can extricate him.

Flying inverted less than 50 feet above the ground, aerobatic pilot Art Scholl cuts a ribbon held aloft.

3

In the old days when all men in flying machines were considered magnificent, it seemed a mad, mad thing to engage in "looping the loop and defying the ground," as a recent song puts it. Even today, "looping the loop" conjures up to many people a sense of tempting the outer limits of fate. Yet looping is the simplest form of aerobatics, which is the art of contortioning an airplane through maneuvers that seem to defy the possibilities of aerodynamics. To a pilot attempting a loop for the first time—if he is sane, he will have an instructor aboard—it is still daring to dive a plane at the earth, then to bring up the nose higher and higher and then over and over until he is looking *up* at the earth and watching the horizon move backward and upward as the plane comes around and dives again. After he masters it with the instructor aboard, it is still daring for him to try it alone, and especially to try it alone a second time if the first attempt fails and the plane stalls or rolls out into what seems like the beginning of a fall from the sky. And that is just the beginning, for there are rolls to master and such thrills as hammerheads and Immelmanns and lomcovaks. Daring.

One can do these maneuvers for the sheer fun of momentary horror or for a sense of perfect control, and one can do it for a living. Flying stunt men are rare birds—for good reason. The smoke issuing from the World War I Fokker Triplane that your favorite movie hero has shot down may be chemical, but the death-dive of the Hun is actually happening. In fact, stunt men have often been contracted not only to crash airplanes but to crash them upside down, or into trees *just so*, and to get it right the first time—airplanes cost money—or no payment. So these consummate pilots fly their dangerous missions for demanding (non-pilot) directors, and if it means some hard bumps, well that's showbiz. Daring.

One can be daring in the skies even without benefit of airplane, except for getting up to a few thousand feet above that hard ground. It is possible to live out that universal nightmare of falling from an impossible height, of falling and falling until waking up saves one from the terrible end. The real-life counterpart to waking up is pulling the ripcord of one's parachute, assuming one remembers not to be hypnotized by the spectacle of the ever-so-slowly rising ground to the point where the parachute can be no help. It is possible to

Trailing chemical smoke, a stunt pilot can turn flight into epic action.

test one's nerve to the fullest, in slow motion, by sitting in a jump plane, trussed up in jump suit and parachutes, waiting out the takeoff, the climb to altitude, and the jumps of one's companions until there is nothing left but to chicken out or climb out with intent to fall into nothingness. Daring.

Here is how derring-do is done.

1. Aerobatics

WE build and fly our airplanes as if they were cars—or, worse, buses and trains. But the spirit of adventure, though hidden, is often present even in sedate pilots and sedate airplanes, for it is a delight to bend into figures and filigree the long, straight line of ordinary flight.

Every bank is a roll begging to come to life; every pull-up is full of yearning for the loop it might become. Federal regulators have given the name "aerobatics" to all maneuvers involving more than 60 degrees of bank or 45 degrees of climb; but in the mind of the pilot who is at home in aerobatics, there is no such arbitrary line between the certifiedly safe and the automatically perilous. An airplane seems no better suited for turning level than for pulling up into a steep wingover so that the earth slides momentarily over the top of the canopy as speed is lost and then revolves smoothly back into place as speed is regained; a spiraling descent seems no more natural a movement than a casual barrel roll.

Precipitous flight maneuvers may terrify and even sicken the uninitiated passenger, but the aerobatic pilot is no Superman; he is merely a complete pilot. His or her knowledge of the capabilities and qualities of an airplane and his intimacy with the intricate and spacious geometry of the wheeling air make him at home upside down, weightless, tumbling downward, or sailing straight up with no earth in sight. One's mind does not grasp

OPPOSITE. The secret of a good loop is keeping the wings level as you come over the top.

desperately at instants in the airplane's course, seeking a familiar orientation; it flies with the airplane, unconsciously appreciating rates of acceleration and deceleration, accumulations and dissipations of momentum, exchanges of potential and kinetic energy. Just as a confident walker crosses a stream on a narrow log with unhesitating, rapid steps, while another, faltering, loses balance and stumbles, the aerobatic pilot lives in and feels the motion and state of the airplane, making his adjustments in full swing, while the uninitiated would hesitate, wonder, fear, and fall.

The joy of it is in the speed, the variety, the flow, the anticipation and fulfillment. A pilot who has learned aerobatics has won his airplane, illuminating flight's dark corners and erasing its question marks.

One of the United States' outstanding aerobatic pilots, Ed Mahler, in his PJ biplane.

Come along with us now for a tour of the upside-down world. Close your eyes and try to imagine—or perhaps remember—how those maneuvers feel; consider the elation and mastery of it. This is aviation's ultimate game.

In aerobatic flying, the focus is on trying to make a mass of half a ton cavort in the air like a bird. The techniques are unnatural; the sensations, at least initially, uncomfortable. Some of the airplanes most readily available for aerobatics are those worst suited for them: high-wing, tandem two-seaters with closed cockpits and sluggish control responses. But once a pilot knows the techniques of aerobatics, has confidence in his airplane, and is advanced to a point where he can go solo in single-seat biplanes and low-wingers, he finds himself tremendously enjoying maneuvers which, a little while before, seemed more likely to turn him away from the sport.

The main obstacle to overcome is anxiety. This cannot be eliminated consciously; only habit and a growing confidence in the airplane can dissipate the feeling of helplessness that overcomes you when you first see the horizon keel over and fall away before you. Anxiety causes disorientation, motion sickness, and the tension that make aerobatics exhausting for a novice. It interferes with your sense of timing in strange ways, depriving you of the relaxed and rhythmic intuition of speeds and dynamics which unifies and mellows the performance of the professionals. Anxiety and tension make you focus on individual instants rather than on continuums of instants; you run short of what pilots call "rate information"—information about how fast things are happening, and therefore about when speed, altitude, or attitude will reach some unacceptable value. To do good aerobatics, you have to be able to compare the rates of change of speed, angle, and altitude; at the top of a loop, for instance, you have to adjust the rate of pitch change (that is, of the nose moving up or down across the horizon) to make up for the changes in the speed of the airplane, if the loop is to appear circular from the ground. Most loops are narrower than they are tall because the pilot forgets that as he coasts slowly over the top of the loop, he has to relax for a while on the stick and not hurry the airplane over the hump.

Unfortunately, anxiety cannot be dissolved by an effort of will; habit is

the best solvent for it. Suppose, though, that you could get into an aerobatic airplane for the first time relaxed and confident. Rather than rack the airplane into a maneuver and then hang on like grim death until it comes out, as most novices do, you could consciously fly it all the time, knowing at every moment what is going to happen over the next string of moments. Here's how you would fly through a few of the basic maneuvers. *This is meant only as a general description, not as instruction. No pilot should try doing aerobatics unless at first accompanied by a qualified instructor.*

The spin is not usually considered an aerobatic maneuver, but recognizing a spin and knowing how to recover from one is fundamental to all kinds of flying, although spins have been removed from the list of maneuvers which an applicant for a pilot's license must learn to perform, on the principle that it is better simply to learn to avoid spins altogether.

Your first spin is always an eye-opener. You slow the airplane down to a few miles an hour above stalling speed with the engine idling. The nose is high above the horizon and the airplane may feel somewhat unsteady. With a smooth, rapid movement, you pull the stick all the way back into your lap and simultaneously push one rudder pedal fully forward. The stick stays back and centered. In most airplanes, you have to hold the rudder pedal down hard for the spin to continue. First, the nose pitches up, and then the airplane keels over to the side on which you are holding the rudder. The nose falls past the horizon until it's pointing almost straight down. At the same time, a rotating movement begins. In most aerobatic airplanes, the spin stabilizes immediately; you look straight down at the landscape as it revolves rapidly. The altimeter unwinds at a high rate. This is the "deadly tailspin" featured in old movies and bellowed about by air show announcers. Actually, it's not deadly at all, so long as the airplane and pilot are ready for it. Neutral rudder and a quick, small, forward movement of the stick stop the rotation and unstall the wings; the airplane immediately settles into a steep dive at low speed, from which you recover gradually, taking care not to pull up too sharply and restall the wings.

The loop is probably the simplest of maneuvers—though, like many simple acts, it is difficult to do perfectly. You usually start by lining up on a road, just for reference, although staying precisely on an axis is not at first especially important. You enter a shallow dive and pick up speed until your indicated airspeed is about 20 percent above normal cruise. You may have to throttle back to keep from overspeeding the engine, except in some of the newer aerobatic ships, which have constant-speed props. Note the altitude at which you begin your pull-up. As you pull up, you push the throttle gradually forward. There is a feeling of being under the influence of a strong but not uncomfortable G-force. The ailerons and rudder remain centered, unless the

The loop.

airplane begins to wander from a steady path. You see your airspeed dropping rapidly as you climb toward the top of the loop. You'll be fascinated by the rapid movement of the needle toward the stalling speed, but if you can tear yourself away, it's good to glance out to the side to get a sense of the rate of rotation of the horizon. As you come over the top, level and inverted, you should have enough speed left to be holding just enough G to keep you comfortably in your seat. If you're running out of speed, it's not a big problem: just gently ease up on the back pressure until you feel light in your seat, since an unloaded wing can't stall. Looking up and back now, you see the horizon coming up above and behind you. Don't rush the loop: you're going slowly now, and the nose should merely coast downward as the speed begins to pick up and you again back off the throttle. Keep the wings level, increasing the back pressure as you pass the vertical. If you have done everything correctly, you should level out at the altitude at which you started and feel the satisfying jolt of passing through your own wake.

A well-executed loop is a study in smooth and timely transitions. It is not a maneuver in which you first finish one step and then begin another. The G-forces face and accumulate with changes in speed, and the rate of change of pitch angle should ideally alter in precise inverse proportion to the speed. It is impossible to judge the roundness of a loop from inside the airplane, until you have had a friend watch from the ground and comment often enough to give you an idea of what a round loop really feels like. On the other hand, an unrefined loop is lots of fun and easy—it was the first aerobatic maneuver ever performed.

Slow roll.

The roll has several forms, of which the most easily performed is the barrel roll. You can do a barrel roll at cruising speed. The nose is pulled up above the horizon as though to begin a loop, and then full aileron is applied to one side or the other, along with enough opposite rudder to keep the nose pointing straight ahead. The airplane will rotate, and the nose will describe a circle more or less tangential to the horizon. If the airplane was pitched up to the proper degree before beginning the roll, it will be in level inverted flight at the top but still pulling positive G—so there's no problem of hanging from your seat belt or disturbing the dust on the floor of the cabin. Since a barrel roll involves no unusual strain on the airplane, any airplane can do one—though only approved types can do them legally. The danger of blowing the maneuver and ending up pulling excessive loads makes it inadvisable for a novice to try to roll a standard-category airplane. The problem to avoid is letting the nose drop too low during the inverted part of the roll. If you get into the beginning of an inverted dive, you "dish out" of the roll and may get going awfully fast before you fully recover. If the nose is dropping as you come over the top, relax back pressure on the stick—but don't push it sharply forward, since that could lead to an inverted snap roll.

A barrel roll is so called because it describes a path around the outside of a cylinder; it is also called an "aileron roll" because the ailerons are the only controls necessary to perform it. A harder type of roll is the "slow roll," in which the airplane describes a straight line through the air. In a slow roll to the right, the ailerons are held to the right throughout the maneuver. The stick begins in a neutral position, moves forward as the airplane goes over onto its

back in order to keep the nose from dropping below the horizon, and returns to neutral as the airplane passes through the wings-vertical position. Meanwhile, the rudder first assists the ailerons in getting the roll going; then it goes against the ailerons in order to hold the nose up on the horizon during the wings-vertical, or "knife-edge," flight, this time in the same direction as the ailerons; it finally returns to neutral as the airplane rolls out into level flight.

The trick here is mainly in keeping the nose on the horizon. It's hard at first because you tend to respond by sudden exaggerated control movements when you notice that the nose is going off the point; with practice, though, the flow of control movements becomes familiar and corrections become instinctive. When you have the control flow in the slow roll in hand, you can try hesitation rolls, which come in four-point, eight-point, and sixteen-point varieties, with the roll stopping sharply at points all the way around, so that the feeling of the maneuver is polygonal rather than circular.

When you can do a slow roll without strain at moderate airspeeds, you can do a neat Immelmann turn, while in a half roll at the top of a loop; and, with a little more effect, a Cuban eight, which involves two partial back-to-back loops connected by half rolls executed at a 45-degree angle to the ground, so that the whole maneuver describes a figure eight lying on its side.

Another easy sort of roll is the snap roll, which is entered like a spin but from a speed about 20 mph above the stall. For a right snap, for instance, full right rudder and full back stick make the airplane spin at a surprising

Snap roll.

rate—much faster than it would if the wing weren't stalled. Opposite control applied about a quarter turn before the end of the roll brings the airplane out. Usually, you can snap nicely without the aid of any aileron for entry, though an aileron is normally necessary to stop the roll. Snap rolls are hard on airplanes, and different planes snap in different ways. It may take some work to get the best snap out of each type—though in airplanes with American engines, it helps to snap to the left, because you then have torque helping you around. Snap rolls are very easy once you have the entry and recovery down, since no control manipulation is necessary during the roll; you just kick the airplane into the roll and, when the time comes, kick it back out.

The hammerhead is a timing maneuver. Again, having someone watching on the ground to criticize your performance helps. You start as you would for a loop, with perhaps a little less speed; you pull up until the fuselage is vertical, and then hold it in a vertical climb, making sure the wings stay square with the world. Just before you run out of airspeed, you kick the left rudder. The airplane will cartwheel over to the left. At the same time, the fact that one wing is moving faster than the other will make the plane want to rotate about its roll axis. A little opposite aileron stops the roll, and you end up with neutralized controls, facing straight down; you then recover as from a loop. Like the loop, the hammerhead is easy in principle but difficult to execute with finesse. Start with left hammerheads since, in American airplanes, the rotating prop helps you to cartwheel to the left.

OPPOSITE. Hammerhead.

When you have these basic maneuvers down, practice them as much as you can. Nothing helps aerobatics as much as the kind of relaxed and unconscious manipulation of the controls that comes when habit wears tension away. Eventually, you find yourself becoming more and more aware of the big picture you are drawing in the sky. As maneuvers become more natural to you, you concentrate less on their details and more on their broad rhythms and on the most elegant and economical exchanges of energy and momentum. It takes time, and not all pilots find it congenial; but for those who do, few pleasures match that of riding a little open cockpit airplane through the sky, out-maneuvering the birds.

There are two styles of aerobatic flying for the pilot who has gotten past the stage of merely surviving each maneuver. One is the precise and demanding style of competition, in which all maneuvers are to be performed within a limited volume of air, or box, with perfect precision. The emphasis here is on good geometry and tight flying, on holding accurate axes and eliminating irrelevant loose ends—such as the tail-wag that sometimes follows a hammerhead, or a slight overshoot and return on a snap roll. The other style is that of air show aerobatics—a slam-bang approach in which the impression of danger and stress is valued above precision of execution, although precision is still a matter of pride to the pilots.

Air show aerobatics are the only type most people ever see. They are invariably accompanied by the ravings of an announcer who sees it as his duty to whip the crowd into a frenzy of fear and admiration, and to keep talking even when he has almost no idea of what is actually going on.

Usually, air show pilots equip their planes with devices that trail smoke, sometimes brightly colored, behind them, marking their passage and producing queer effects when, during a tailslide, the plane seems to disappear into its own cloudy wake. Air show smoke dissipates rapidly; it stays long enough to provide a hint as to the path of the airplane, but not long enough to reveal the inaccuracies of square loops whose last corner is quite round.

OPPOSITE. Smoke traces part of an aerobatic routine. The pilot has just done a vertical snap roll capped by a hammerhead.

Colored ropes of smoke from wing tips braid themselves into intricate pigtails as the tip vortices seize and twist them.

    The air show pilot prefers five sloppy snap rolls in fast succession to one perfect one. He deals in extremes. It does not matter so much if a loop is round, so long as the pullout occurs within 20 feet of the runway. Some of them—Art Scholl particularly—see the illusion of impending disaster as their best drawing card.

Art Scholl climbs inverted in his Chipmunk.

The act begins with a roll after takeoff and an inverted climbout at a 45-degree angle to the runway heading. The pilot rolls out in the distance, gains height rapidly, then turns inbound, aligned with the runway, and dives to gain speed. At mid-field, he pulls sharply upward and climbs vertically, with a four-point hesitation roll on the way up. The top of his 1,000-foot climb is crowned with a hammerhead. He dives, recovers inverted, and then it's a three-quarter outside loop with an outside snap roll on the recovery. The maneuvers follow hard and fast, with dizzying profusion and violence.

Sometimes, the climax of the act is a non-maneuver called the "lomcovak," which begins with a climbing outside snap roll and ends differently each time. The airplane is out of control during this maneuver and does more or less what it likes. Usually, a tumbling, cartwheeling movement occurs, with the airplane wreathed in smoke. One does not, under any circumstances, expect to see an airplane flip end over end in quite this way.

Lomcovak.

The lomcovak was unique in its oddness and unpredictability for a long time, though now other pilots are discovering other ways of doing the impossible. One of them has dreamed up a maneuver in which the plane briefly stands up on its tail and moves horizontally along its own vertical axis—a momentary but astonishing display; and a certain Englishman is said to have perfected a way of using differential power in a twin-engine jet to make a plane do a 540-degree hammerhead—a hammerhead with one full rotation around the yaw axis thrown in for good measure.

Air show maneuvers are chosen because they play well; some of them are not especially difficult, but they make a greater impression on an audience, especially a non-flying one, than some competition maneuvers that are of extraordinary difficulty. Such a maneuver is the rolling turn, in which four successive slow rolls are performed while the airplane makes a full-circle track along the ground. This is a profoundly confusing and incomprehensible maneuver when one first experiences it; it is almost equally confusing to watch, and so one rarely sees it in air shows. To an uninitiated onlooker, it appears that the airplane is merely corkscrewing erratically and going nowhere.

Another element of competition aerobatics that is less important in air show work is the use of outside maneuvers. Non-flyers don't realize how unnatural inverted flight feels to the pilot, or how difficult it sometimes is to keep everything under control while one's hair is standing on end and the blood is rushing to one's head. Outside maneuvers look pretty much like inside ones from the ground; it's usually only the pilots who gasp with admiration when a difficult outside maneuver is performed.

Inverted flight is indispensable to any aerobatic pilot, though; and so, if you want to go beyond merely familiarizing yourself with the basic aerobatic maneuvers, you have to get used to flying upside down. Most airplanes are not equipped to do it for more than a short time, since fuel and oil stop feeding to the engine. One solution to this problem is simply to let the engine stop, and glide for some time in the inverted position at a high altitude, practicing turns, climbs, and descents. Your seat belt, by the way, has to be extremely tight; if it is merely tight, you will end up hanging from it, off the seat, and will have trouble with your rudder control. Another solution is to get an airplane with capability for inverted flight—though it will rent for more than one without that capability.

You'll find that inverted flight will make the blood run to your head, and that your capacity to tolerate inverted acceleration will probably be less than your capacity to tolerate it right side up—which is also true of the airplane itself. Extreme and prolonged positive G produces loss of vision, as

French Air Force Magisters demonstrating precision aerobatics.

does somewhat less extreme inverted G. The vision returns in a few seconds, and some fliers accept its coming and going as a routine part of doing aerobatics; but most pilots feel more comfortable if they can see where they're going all the time.

Since there's no particular reason for pursuing one style of aerobatics rather than another, you'll find yourself drawn to competition precision, air show flamboyance, or just plain horsing around in accordance with your personality and tastes. There are plenty of snobs waiting to put you down if you don't strive for, or attain, perfection, but the whole point of flying for fun is to have fun. You have only yourself to please, and you can go on at your own pace, inventing your own routines and assessing your own limitations. Do it any way you like, but remember, if you haven't done it upside down, you haven't really done it.

Several nonmilitary aircraft are well capable of performing aerobatics, but a few among them have become especially preferred due to their excellent performance. One is the favorite of a group known as the Red Devils.

The Red Devils are a dose of sound and fury that shatters the mind and leaves the senses reeling. Part rowdy carnival display, part skilled technical exhibition, their show is one of the world's premier aerobatic acts. This is because the team is made up of an élite trio of aerobatic pilots—Charlie Hillard, Gene Soucy, and Tom Poberezny—all one-time U.S. national champions and one world champion. It is also because they fly the world's top aerobatic machines—the Pitts Specials.

The ease with which the three identical Red Devils perform the most intricate, wrenching maneuvers suggests that they are endowed with the latest aerodynamics science can provide. Yet the Pitts Special is basically a 1945 design that has undergone more than three decades of refinement.

It is the most ancient concept: a wooden-wing biplane with welded tubular fuselage frame, and the entire skeleton covered with fabric—plain and simple. The most dramatic improvements made to this airplane during its entire history are the addition of a double set of ailerons (four instead of two) and the incorporation of a symmetrical airfoil. The double ailerons increased

The Pitts Special in, for it, a conventional position.

the rate of roll, and the symmetrical airfoil improved inverted or so-called outside maneuvers.

The popularity of the airplane is such now that demonstration teams not only in the United States but in Canada and Great Britain have adopted the Pitts for air show work where maximum melodrama is called for. An extra undeniable attraction is the fact that a Pitts Special won the team and the men's and women's world aerobatic championship for the United States at the last world aerobatic competition, held in Salon de Provence, France, in the summer of 1972.

Things were not always so rosy for the Pitts. Both at the preceding meet in 1970 in Hullavington, England, and later in France, the little biplane

The Yak 18, the Pitts's Russian archrival.

was held in rather low esteem on the international aerobatic circuit. "Old-fashioned, archaic" were the disparaging comments of the other pilots. In England, the champion to beat was the Czechoslovakian Zlin, which had racked up an impressive record of aerobatic victories around Europe.

A closed cockpit, low-wing monoplane, the Zlin represented what everybody felt was the trend of the future. Aerobatic judges had become so accustomed to the flying characteristics of the Zlin and its Russian counterpart, the Yak 18, that the Pitts Special flew under a special handicap. It flew "oddly," and its small size, compared with that of other aircraft, gave the judges scale problems.

Then, at France, the favorite of the experts was the sophisticated Swiss-German Akrostar of Arnold Wagner.

In spite of all this, the Pitts Special not only showed it could hold its own among the world's best; it beat the wheel pants off them, capturing the men's team title in England and repeating this feat at France, while adding the men's and women's individual titles. Thus, Charlie Hillard and Mary Gaffaney became the world champs—in Pitts Specials. And old Paw (Curtis) Pitts, the builder, became the designer laureate of the competition circuit.

No mass-production factory aircraft was his, but a handcrafted machine that had enjoyed little more than experimental status for most of its history. It was a genuine homebuilt design, in that plans were sold by mail order to anybody who wanted to try his hand at constructing one.

Later on, as the popularity of the design spread, Curtis Pitts, in Homestead, Florida, sank a small fortune into getting FAA certification for the aircraft so it could be sold from the shop as a finished product. He also got certified a new, stretched two-place trainer, the S-2, and, to provide the best of both worlds, he supplied complete aircraft kits for people who wished to avoid the nuisance of scrounging their own components but still wanted to build their own aircraft.

How can so antique a design lead the world in aerobatic performance? Easy: with 180 hp (200 hp for the S-2) and a gross weight of only 1,150 pounds (less than a Cessna 150's 1,600 pounds), it has the power-to-weight ratio to perform the vertical climbing maneuvers called for in formal aerobatic competition without losing momentum.

What makes the Pitts eminently responsive in aerobatics makes it a challenge to land. On flaring, the pilot must work to keep the plane heading straight as he eases into a three-point touchdown.

On the other hand, the drag provided by the double wing, with all its wires and struts, and by the fixed landing gear, gives the pilot a natural speed brake for diving maneuvers. The small size and effective double ailerons supply astonishing controllability and rapid response unequaled by other aerobatic aircraft. And the symmetrical airfoil makes inverted flying a cinch.

If there is one flaw in the Pitts's makeup, it's the kind that adds to the aircraft's charisma. The airplane is a strange, hot-landing, squirrel-like machine that requires a sure touch and constant attention to avoid ground looping. First of all, the pilot sits so low in the fuselage that he can barely peek above the rim of the cockpit. This is supposed to allow an ideal visual reference for precision aerobatics almost along the longitudinal axis of the airplane. But, on landing, as the nose is raised, runway visibility becomes nonexistent, and peripheral vision is paramount for the pilot who would try to gauge a perfect three-point tail-dragger touchdown.

The flier who achieves it, however, is assured a reputation as an authentic hot pilot.

If the lineage of the Pitts Special seems to go back to the remote past of aeronautical design, the Pitts has a partner in the Bellanca Champion Decathlon. The latter can trace its parentage back to the Aeronca Champion of several decades ago. Unlike the Pitts, however, it started life with more modest aspirations for aerobatic stardom. As the Champ of the forties, it served nobly as a kind of trainer and personal two-seat puddle-jumper.

Years later, under the aegis of the Bellanca Corporation, it evolved into an inexpensive aerobatic trainer named the Citabria (spell it backward and you'll see why). And in 1971, it was slicked up and improved for competition aerobatics, and called the Decathlon.

Whereas the Decathlon has never challenged the Pitts in the arena of unlimited professional aerobatics, it nicely fills a niche as a relatively inexpensive production trainer with pleasant aerobatic handling qualities.

The Decathlon, and the Citabria for that matter, have at least one

OPPOSITE. The Bellanca Citabria, which begat the competition Decathlon.

advantage over the Pitts. They are both perfectly straightforward, ground-handling aircraft that offer the pilot a good view of the runway for taxi, takeoff, and landing. Neither exhibits any tendency toward ground looping, and both can handle strong crosswinds with little difficulty.

Once in the air, however, the Decathlon exhibits a marked improvement over the Citabria in handling qualities. It has a shorter wingspan to increase the rate of roll and a nearly symmetrical airfoil for better inverted flight. Aileron chords were increased and control surface gaps sealed for better effectiveness. The aircraft also was given a constant-speed prop to simplify engine monitoring during maneuvers.

To appreciate the flying qualities of the Decathlon, it helps to take a trial flight in its predecessor, the Citabria. The Citabria, which for some years had the distinction of being the only U.S. production aircraft certified for aerobatic flight, has serious shortcomings where any but the most basic maneuvers are involved.

Control pressures are extremely heavy, and inverted flight is a real chore. The problem with introducing the art of aerobatics to student pilots in this kind of airplane is that the plane exaggerates the difficulties and discourages further aerobatic training.

By contrast, the Decathlon has a modified control system with less friction and greatly lightened stick forces. The rate of roll in the Decathlon is about twice that of a Citabria. And inverted flight, which can quickly go awry as either a stall or a dive in a Citabria, is a joy in the Decathlon, even to the extent of allowing hands-off flight when trimmed up properly.

Strengthened in the empennage (tail) area to take the stress of violent aerobatics, the Decathlon represents a quantum jump above its sister plane. Multiple snap rolls, tailslides, recovery forward and backward, hammerheads, and rolling 360-degree turns are all well within the capabilities of the aircraft—as are the jolting, end-over-end lomcovaks.

Since the 150-hp airplane weighs 1,800 pounds at gross compared with 1,150 pounds for the 180-hp one-seater Pitts Special, it suffers from lack of oomph in climbing maneuvers like square loops and vertical point rolls. But the Decathlon's closed cockpit, attractive decor, and cross-country cruising speed of over 130 mph combine to make the aircraft a useful, pleasant all-around sport aircraft, trainer, and touring ship.

The Czechs, performing some kind of aeronautical magic, have come up with one of the great classic sport aircraft of all time: the Zlin Z-526 series. Such was its reputation as an aerobatic ship that it struck fear into the hearts of competitors from other countries for years. The aircraft rode a wave of popularity that finally dissolved with the rude shock of a series of disastrous structural failures and the hell-for-leather assault of the American Pitts biplanes.

Aside from bringing home an entire silver cabinet full of trophyware for Czech aerobatic pilots in the 1960s, the Zlin has had a role in some poignant aerial dramas.

English aerobatic ace Neil Williams added a complete chapter to aviation daring and quick thinking under stress in a Zlin when a lower bolt in one wing separated, causing the wing to bend up and threaten to rupture completely. Flying without a parachute, the Englishman turned the airplane inverted to reverse the pressure on the wing, then worked his way back to the

The clipped-wing Zlin, as flown by the East German team at the world aerobatic meet in 1972.

airport, flew the pattern upside down, and at the last second rolled upright to land safely.

In another incident, the very first world aerobatic champion, Czech Ladislav Bezak, crammed his entire family of wife and five kids into the front seat of his two-seat Zlin and then dodged a Mig-17 jet interceptor in a wild escape flight to Germany in the winter of 1971.

It was the superb pilot Bezak, incidentally, who invented the lomcovak, and he did it in the Zlin. And, of course, it was in a Zlin that he won that first world competition at Bratislava, Czechoslovakia, in 1960. Zlin pilots also won the world meets again in 1962, 1964, and 1968. Little wonder the aircraft was held in such awe in aerobatic circles during the sixties.

OPPOSITE. A favorite among pilots for sentimental as well as aerodynamic reasons is the Bücker Jungmeister, here flown by the late Bevo Howard, one of the finest aerobatic pilots in the history of the sport.

Until the advent of the American Pitts, the Zlin and Yak 18 (its Soviet counterpart) dominated world competition.

As far as handling qualities are concerned, the Zlin displays elegant control lightness, but requires rather longer stick movements than the Pitts. As the Pitts began to come into its heyday in 1970, the Zlin revealed shortcomings in its ability to do knife-edge flight (a cinch in the Pitts) and to perform vertical climbing maneuvers without running out of power.

The Zlin engines were usually inline, inverted six-cylinder powerplants of no more than 160 hp in the early sixties; and, with over a ton of gross weight to move around, they soon found themselves at a disadvantage in the potent company of the Pitts. Later, 180-hp and 200-hp powerplants were incorporated into the Zlin lines.

One interesting technical characteristic of the Zlins is their use of a novel form of automatic constant-speed prop over which the pilot has no control. The pilot need only set the throttle, and prop speed is determined automatically.

The Zlin line had its inception way back in 1948 when the Zlin 26 appeared as a primary trainer, powered with a little 105-hp Walter Minor engine. It was succeeded by the Zlin 126 Trener II, which in 1955 gave way to the Zlin 226 with a 160-hp Walter Minor 6-III engine. The last version of the Zlin to appear was the 526 AFS, with a 35 percent faster rate of roll and wings shortened from 35 feet to slightly over 29 feet in span.

The factory in Otrokovice also designed a 200-hp Lycoming-powered model called the Zlin 526-L, and expressed interest in obtaining U.S. certification. But so far none has been forthcoming, and pilots who purchase the rare thoroughbred Zlin aircraft must do so with the understanding that the airplane can fly only with the *experimental* tag in this country.

Will the Czechs return to the aerobatic eminence they once held with an improved new line of the old standby that served as aeroclub trainer and glider tow for so many years? Only time will tell.

CHAPTER

2. *Showman*

MANY years ago, a brilliant observer of American culture, Joseph Wood Krutch, pointed out that the way we see the world—both its reality and our illusions about it—is shaped by what we see in the movies. Even in the late 1920s and early 1930s, there were signs that real members of the underworld were beginning to imitate crooks they saw on the screen. By the time Edward G. Robinson, Humphrey Bogart, and George Raft had made some gangland features, a sizable number of hoods had taken on the Robinson voice, the Bogart lisp, or the Raft toss of the coin.

Things haven't changed. Only add television to the movies as an influence on the way we see and act and aviation to crime as one of several activities so colored. Ever since *Wings* was first released in 1929, Americans, especially young Americans, have built their ideas of the romance of flying from days—notably Saturday afternoons—and evenings watching airplanes of all vintages being wrenched through the skies in assaults on the barriers of time and space and, more than occasionally, in assaults upon each other. Many a budding sport flier has watched a racing plane, a looping plane, a gliding plane, or other dramatically performing aircraft with his eyes on the ship and at least part of his memory careening through the void bearing such heroes as Cary Grant, Gary Cooper, Humphrey Bogart (this time as a test pilot), or William Holden to glory, doom, love, or court-martial.

Hollywood may be a kingdom of make-believe, but unless the airplanes doing those crazy things on film are models—and seldom do models look like anything but models—they are real planes flown by real pilots facing real

Frank Tallman—very much the Hollywood image of the intrepid pilot.

Sometimes a film can create curious combinations. Here, a very properly dressed Tallman checks a very antique airplane before flying it, a vintage 1910 Blériot.

dangers to create the "illusion" of danger. These pilots fly at great speeds, put their planes through outlandish maneuvers, aim their machines around, at, and nearly through other machines—and all to please directors and cameramen who usually have little idea how much a test of skill and nerves such flying is. The most daring elements of sport flying are there, but these pilots are engaged in serious business—in terms of the risks, one of the most serious of businesses.

Frank Tallman is the foremost of movie stunt pilots. What most aviators experience only in nightmares, Tallman does for a living. When he isn't planning or executing some daredevil trick, he can often be found in his office, feet on the desk, his suntanned hands maneuvering in the air as he reminisces about funny or terrifying incidents that lie behind the aerial thrills and chills moviegoers are *supposed* to see.

Tallman has more tales of flying to tell, perhaps, than anyone else alive, and more will to tell them. If you spent three rainy days in a boondocks hangar with Tallman waiting for the clouds to lift, you'd leave with a full heart and a sore ear; he is a raconteur with a vengeance, a Niagara of anecdotes, a Pandora's Box of bizarre accidents, bewildering malfunctions, hair-raising stunts, false alarms, discursive nostalgias, amazing revelations, and unexpected quirks. He is a catalogue of hierarchies and genealogies of airplanes, flights, voyages, disasters planned and unplanned, all strung together in a chain of dovetailing associations without beginning or, apparently, end.

Most of the airplane footage you see in movies—except, of course, for stock footage of airplanes just cruising along—is staged by Tallman and his colleagues. His work extends from the routine (staging a "non-pilot-finds-him-self-at-the-controls" sequence, for example) to the spectacular (flying a Seabee through a house, a biplane down the central street of a stage town, a twin Beech through a billboard, or a Grumman Duck so close to the Orinoco treetops that he comes back with branches hanging from the landing gear and one wing partially severed). He and his men executed the memorable B-25 formation takeoff that opened *Catch-22*, and though he bemoans the exclusion of most of the airplane footage from the film, what is there is extraordinary enough: eighteen hulking, angular bombers, compressed by the long lens and

The Great Waldo Pepper demanded great flying from Tallman and his colleagues. In the film, Pepper's rival loses his wheels on takeoff. Two planes were used for the stunt. One was pancaked into a lake, the other, used for the takeoff shot, was landed *very gently* on tiny wheels just visible at the ends of the landing gear struts.

blurred by the waves of heat rising from the ground, taxiing three abreast onto the runway, running up their thirty-six engines, and then rolling out, wave following wave, rising from the ground and seeming to float and flutter in the rippling air, creeping almost motionlessly away from the telescopic camera like mounting doves.

"We were coming in on six and eight in echelon," so Tallman describes it, "and just making fighter breakups in this big airplane, pitching up, pitching way up almost over on your back and following it right through with a fighter turn all the way in to a landing. That's the way we flew it all the time. And you're flying out over the Gulf of Cortez with a lot of sharks. You splash one out there and chances are you're not going to get home. And you hit in midair, hit in midair with one of these -25s, forget it, you don't even have time to tell your beads. Some of it was wildly dangerous. We made 18-plane takeoffs on a strip half as wide as the one out there. And if anybody blows you've just had it. We had to tell the guys, 'Look fellows, if it looks like you're gonna lose an engine or something, get it off the runway no matter what you have to do. Because it's the only chance of life for everybody behind you.' We made takeoffs the likes of which I've never seen and will never be recorded again. Because danger! Past the first four or five airplanes, they had everything they could do to maintain that airplane straight ahead. With full strength there must be 500 pounds of effort on those controls to hold that airplane straight ahead. Because it is being bucked by 50,000 horsepower of wind. And those takeoffs were something else. They made anything done in the war look like kid stuff. And not a bit of it appears. . . ."

In another scene for *Catch-22*, the real-life situation became bizarre. As Tallman tells it:

"In the story, the guy who doesn't like Yossarian getting at his girl friend on the beach dives at him with an old L-5, and there's a photographer out on the raft whom he doesn't see till it's too late and he hits him and kills him, busts him in half, that's part of the story. I flew it with a Stinson L-5 and I had a steel prop on it and had it rigged so I could cut this dummy and you know you got a close shot of the real guy, then they take him away and substitute a dummy there. And the dummy was magnificently made, I mean it was articulated and the dummy had a Leica camera made of balsa wood, beautifully done. I cut cardboard silhouettes and I cut the real dummies and tried them out at different angles and speeds. And the last one I came zooming in and hit this guy right on cue and he dissolved, you know, and you feel a hell of a thunk as the airplane hits this dummy and then I'm right on about three feet off the water heading into the Gulf of Mexico and ease back on the stick and nothing happens. Pull back and the stick is absolutely locked. So I just get both hands on this thing and give one godawful heave, at which point the stick unlocks and I get some climb, but I don't get much movement. So I trim out and get high enough, I make—I don't have too much ailerons—so I make a rudder turn very carefully and make a long straight-in to the runway and set down. What had happened was that this dummy's hand had come off at the wrist, flown over the top wing and lit in the elevators, and when I landed, it reads like a ghost story, the hand was locked into the elevators of the airplane. I still have the hand out there in our back office."

Tallman has a wooden leg. He got it in a freak accident on a go-kart, followed by some medical bungling. He leads a charmed life, it seems, perhaps because of the rain of salt he keeps going over both shoulders during meals. Paul Mantz, his partner of many years, was killed in the breakup of the improbable airplane they had cobbled together for an improbable film, *The Flight of the Phoenix*. Tallman learned of it by being awakened by a telephone call from a newspaper reporter looking for a scoop. "Hello, is this Frank Tallman? Have you heard that your partner was killed?" The partner and the leg were lost in quick succession; otherwise, Tallman seems practically unscarred.

He is a tall, slim man of dapper appearance, with a thoroughly scrubbed air; his tanned skin has a luminous clarity, which, with his narrow silver moustache and trim gray hair, makes him look exceedingly like an RAF squadron leader in some Spitfire epic; he lacks only the swagger stick. Tallman

In *Waldo Pepper* the script sometimes called for feigned awkwardness—as when Waldo makes his first attempts at a ground-air boarding of a plane (above)—and always for precision, as during Waldo's dogfight with a German ace (below).

made a film, *Murphy's War*, in the Orinoco with Peter O'Toole, for whom he stood in during the flying sequences; Tallman swears that on the screen you could never tell them apart.

Tallman's office at Orange County Airport is an odd mixture of medieval *objets d'art* and autographed pictures of Thunderbirds, guns, and books. He is a lover of the past, but his capital is in the present. He has flown practically everything there is to fly including Century-Series jet fighters, but he waxes most effusive on the subject of 1940s fighters and the biplanes that preceded them. Jets, with the discipline and automation, the pressure suits, oxygen masks, and jump boots, the hermetic cockpits and the long periods at high G-loads, do not appeal to him. He prefers the near-vertical takeoff of his Boeing F4B1 to a T-38's corkscrew climb out of sight. He likes to lift the Boeing off across the width of a taxiway, while the spectators think he is still taxiing into position. Climb appeals to him in the Bearcat, too, though he has had a couple of unnerving hydraulic failures in the airplane. For sheer, honest flyability, he prefers the P-40 to some of the more prestigious fighters, such as the P-51, of which, unlike almost everyone else, he is not very fond:

"It's just a personal thing with me, I like the P-51 less, for various reasons: one, it's rather heavy on the controls. I'm not talking about being in a war now and running away from somebody and having a really fast airplane, which the P-51, of course, was. I'm talking just simply from the pure pleasure-of-flight standpoint—it's a long way from being a pleasant airplane. I've never seen one of them made comfortable inside, the gosh darned radiator duct comes by underneath your seat and it's throwing heat through there like a stove. Oh, it's the hottest airplane inside you were ever in, you've got to go up to 15,000 or 20,000 feet before you can be comfortable in the damned thing. It's got half the room inside it that the P-40 has. It's much stiffer on the controls than, for example, the P-40 is. The P-40 has a bad directional trim change, but it's nothing you don't get used to, and, of course, your radiator in the P-40 is out where the engine is. So you've got a very comfortable airplane to fly in. And you can roll around a P-51 while the guy's getting the stick over. And with the old-fashioned wing that's on a P-40, it will loop all day, and it's just . . . lovely and sweet and honest. . . . A '51 is the nastiest-looping airplane I ever felt. You've got to do certain things with it and you've got to be used to it before you can get a decent loop out of it. Now a loop is probably the easiest maneuver ever made by anybody aerobatically. The '51 doesn't loop nicely. A Merlin is a cranky miserable engine as far as I'm concerned, everybody else may love it, but I think it's a cranky, miserable engine with 20 times the maintenance you have with an Allison. It doesn't last; for example, the pilot's handbook in the P-51 says you can haul down to 1,500 to 1,600 rpms to get range out of it. I was never able to do it, maybe somebody else was able to. You can take that old Allison in the P-40 and climb up to altitude and haul all the way back so it's indicating 1,400 rpms, you can almost count the blades going by. The thing's only burning 28 gallons an hour and indicating 170 to 175 miles an hour, and it's going like the wind and burning less gas than you burn in a lot of civilian airplanes, way less gas, for instance, than you burn in an AT-6. Sitting there and now when you want it, you can cob that mother

Tallman in a Flying Tiger-painted Curtiss P-40.

and go right on up. When you do that with a Merlin it's going poppety bang! bang! It'll scare the living daylights out of you.

"Maybe everybody thinks that these engines are that good, I think they are, but I've had enough engine failures with almost every kind of powerplant that anybody's ever built. I've had failures in Merlins, failures in Allisons, failures in Wrights, failures in Pratt & Whitneys, failures in Lycomings, failures in Continentals, failures in Le Rhônes, failures in Gnômes. . . .

"The Bearcat is a lovely airplane, but it's another hotbox. That R2800 engine sits close to you, but for performance, nothing else was ever like that. Of course, I hate that downdraft Pratt—that R2800 carburetor on that thing is a regular firebird. Every time, if you miss a start, you've got a fire under that mother and that's miserable, the same thing with the Corsair, you have to be very careful. There's two airplanes that I remember most as being firebirds, they can start a fire just by your looking at them, and that's the Bearcat and a cabin Waco that I had; the Waco YKC Custom had a 245 Jacobs on it and that Jacobs was a great fire engine, particularly in winter time. I would always park in such a way that I could see somebody out in front, because you can never see the fire underneath the cowling, and every time I'd see somebody's horror-stricken face, I'd know we had a fire and I'd chop the throttle and jump out and run around the front with a fire bottle. But for pure performance and certainly one of the loveliest-flying airplanes ever built it's got to be a Bearcat. God, that's a beautiful-flying airplane."

Tallman's amorous enthusiasm for his airplanes is such that in a single conversation, he will call several of them "the loveliest-flying airplane . . ." It isn't dishonesty; it's just that he starts thinking about an airplane and what it feels like, and it gives him a thrill just to think about it and so he lets you know:

"In the air, there never was a lovelier-flying airplane than a P-38. Of all the lovely sounds in an airplane there's none to equal the P-38; that's got to be the ultimate in sounds. And it's got a marvelous sort of sashay movement, because it's such a big airplane that when you roll you can feel those booms kind of rolling around behind you like the tail end of a sled or something. . . ."

In all his years and all his airplanes, Tallman has never bailed out. He was once on a chase-plane job with an early 727, at 35,000 feet in a P-51, and when the work was over, he turned back home and lost the engine during a playful roll off the top of a loop. He could not get it back, and glided down to a safe landing at El Toro Marine Corps Air Station, gingerly turning to final at mid-field and lowering the gear at the last possible instant. For once, he was sweating. You dumb bastard, he said to himself. A few days later, he made some sport parachute jumps, just so that he would know his alternative next time. He says he would cheerfully abandon any of the rare or unique airplanes he flies, rather than dead-stick it into an unpromising field.

The essence of Tallman's work is its variety. He and his fellow pilots must be able to step from a Grumman Duck into a B-25, from the B-25 into a Curtiss Pusher, or an Apache, or a P-51; and in each airplane, they must fly competently, stunt, formate, or cope with emergencies. Tallman distrusts excessive self-confidence in a pilot; he likes a cautious man who sits on the pilot's handbook. He is, in a way, modest about his own abilities:

"I would certainly be no competitor for Art Scholl. Now I'll stunt a Twin Beech or loop or roll a Duck or do other things. But for me to get in and do an international course of aerobatics in the Chipmunk or a Pitts, forget it. I'm not that man at all, because I'd have to spend the same amount of time as Bob Herendeen or Art or maybe a good deal more to qualify with them or be comparable with them. . . ."

Since he is capable of talking unflaggingly for hours about airplanes and the things he has done in them, he ought to qualify as a windbag or a colossal egoist, but he doesn't. He has a gift for talking; rather than eventually keeling over into a deep sleep, his listeners are hypnotized, fascinated, and want to hear more. He is a slow talker, a summer afternoon talker, with his moments of emphasis, his tonal italicizations, punctuating long stretches of disconnected syntax and fervent random associations. No doubt he tells the same stories twice, falls into self-contradiction, waxes careless of his epithets; but those are trivial faults. He is, for all that, a Shakespeare of the hangar yarn, a pilot's pilot who has flown them all, in fact owned them all, who lives for flying, and for whom "cockpit" means not a Naugahyde cell with air conditioning, but a bucket seat and a parachute hanging inside a metal shell, with all its frames and rivets and hydraulic lines exposed to view, wind leaking everywhere, heat from here and cold from there, roars and rushes and moans sometimes, the isolation and languor of a long overwater ferry flight among evening pink cumulus on the way to a movie location. It means sometimes breathlessly careening toward a camera plane, veering off at the last moment; sometimes toward a solid wall (a breakaway wall, a movie wall—but what if it were a trick? Do I have enemies?) swelling ahead to be pierced; sometimes toward the narrow thread of a desert road down below, near it the cluster of glitters and spots of the camera crew, where he is to land a twin-engine bomber—and land it with a bang! because a good landing is nothing, nothing at all on film. He has a sense of airplanes, all times and types, that few men ever have; he is like a scholar who has learned his subject from experience, without degrees. Watch for his credit in movies with airplanes in them. When you see Tallmantz Aviation's name, keep in mind that their job is about the only one in movies in which the behind-the-scenes life is more exciting than what you see on the screen. Gnash your teeth, you who long for romance and derring-do; Tallman's cornered the market.

3. Free Fall

To be so intimate with the wind that it twists your features and claws at your clothes; to be so at the mercy of time and gravity that to miscalculate them even slightly can lead to disaster; to be so daring that you are willing to confront the wind and play at chances with time and space must make you a Superman, right? This is how one jumper would answer that question:

"It's more than a third of my lifetime away now, and I find it difficult to recall much about what got me into skydiving in the first place. I was at Fox Airfield in the desert north of Los Angeles one day with some other people, when a couple of parachutes materialized in the sky. I could hear their characteristic distant rattle. We watched them float to earth. I enthusiastically announced that that was something I'd like to do, and a couple of weeks later, mainly, I suppose, to prove that I had not merely been talking big, I approached the people who ran the jumping operation at Fox. There were two of them: a tall, blond, rather flamboyant fellow and his partner, who was brown-haired, smaller of stature, more reserved, and, I thought, the more serious and important of the two. They invited me over for a $25 indoctrination, which consisted of verbal instruction in the design and use of parachutes, some falling, limp-legged into a sandbox from a 4-foot-high platform, and viewing a bunch of movies of them and their friends in free fall.

"The standard jump course consisted of five static line jumps, meaning that the ripcord that releases the parachute was pulled from the airplane as you fell. After that, you began pulling your own ripcord; first, immediately on

The moment of moments, when the jumper commits himself to empty space.

jumping, and then after delays of increasing length—five seconds, ten, twenty, thirty, forty-five, and finally sixty, the customary maximum. In one minute you would fall about 10,000 feet; the ripcord was supposed to be pulled by the time you were 2,200 feet above the ground. You carried a main chute on the back, a reserve on the chest, and, atop the reserve, an altimeter and a stopwatch, redundant indicators of when to pull. The jump planes were usually four-seat Cessnas, with a small step on the right landing gear leg and no right door. The exit procedure involved turning toward the door while still sitting on the cabin floor, extending your feet until they rested on the step, then reaching out for the wing strut and pulling out until you were standing, slightly crouched, facing the prop. It was important to look forward, not downward, for the stated reason that a stable free-fall position required arching the neck backward; perhaps it was also good not to spend the last few seconds before the jump looking down past your feet at the vertiginously distant earth.

"The instructor, who was called the jumpmaster, would determine when the airplane was over a predetermined point on the ground, slap your shoulder, and shout: 'Go!' He would then lean out the door and watch you drop away. The exit spot was determined initially by dropping a dummy marker and later in the day by the experience of the jumpers, so as to place you more or less in the 'DZ'—drop zone—at Fix, which was a plowed circle 100 or 200 feet across.

"As in every activity requiring physical grace, I was a mediocre student; I went unstable in my first couple of static line jumps, and did six rather than five before being allowed to pull the ripcord myself. Going

Falling through cloud at 3,000 feet. The jumper keeps a sharp eye on his altimeter.

unstable, or going on your back, meant that you neglected to maintain the arched-back, bent-knees, swan dive posture that guaranteed a level, face-down descent, and instead went limp or bent your torso forward so that you rolled over or fell any which way, tumbling, until the explosion of the chute opening yanked you upright. I have one recollection, from my third or fourth jump, of seeing the orange and white stripes of the chute bursting up between my legs, yanking me head over heels with a great wallop that made me see a few small stars on the way down.

"Seeing and recollecting were, at first, intermittent. While out on the step, I saw the horizon, the sky, the side of the airplane, my hands clutching the strut; but of the first few times I have no recollection, after the slap on my shoulder, of seeing anything until the chute had opened and I was sitting in the harness regarding the distant desert at my leisure. I saw nothing; no sky, no ground, no airplane. They were all there, and in later jumps, when I was calmer, I could blandly watch the airplane and the goggle-eyed jumpmaster receding and banking above me, and then shift my attention to the ground, check my spotting, note the altitude, the rapid unwinding of the altimeter and the slow, almost paralytic progress of the stopwatch second hand, all these things registering in good order and in the proportion in which reason places them. Reason, however, had no part in the first jumps, when the fall took place in an instant about which I was later unable to repicture any detail: whether or not I had been stable, whether or not I had counted the seconds loudly—since if the chute didn't open by a slow count of five, you were supposed to go for the reserve—whether the airplane had turned right or left after dumping me, or whether the jumpmaster had waved good-bye.

"I was less terrified during the jump than during the climb, when my mind focused with an awful, concentrated intensity on the receding ground and the approaching jump. When the signal came to get out on the step, I responded mechanically; but once out there, I felt clear, alive, and free of fear. It wasn't what you would expect; the fear did not reach a climax as I stepped out onto that tiny platform. Instead, it vanished. The fall was, at first, an explosion of unconsciousness, the descent in the harness a contemplative pleasure, the landing an exciting bit of derring-do; these satisfactions helped

Baton passing is one of the basic team maneuvers in free falling. Ann Batterson (above left) uses her hands to slow herself as she approaches Marv Steel, who has the baton. As she takes the baton (above), Ann kicks leftward slightly to position herself for the pass. The exchange completed (below), she passes over Marv without touching him.

erase the vividness of the anticipatory fear and made it possible for me to return weekend after weekend to jump again and again. The dread reached a climax well along, at my tenth or fifteenth jump I think, when I spent half a day in the grip of it, making incessant trips to the bathroom. I finally went up with the jumpmaster's assurance that if I didn't want to jump when the moment came, I wouldn't have to. When the moment came, I mechanically climbed out onto the step, the fear vanished, and I jumped.

"I must have had almost twenty jumps when I went to Boston to resume college and got in touch with the skydiving clique there. Eventually, I became the president and sole active member of the Parachute Club, an undergraduate organization whose ranks I pumped up to the required strength of ten by signing aboard all of my friends who were willing to go along with the gag. Some of them went so far as to jump; my roommate and a friend jumped once each, the latter breaking his foot, and a girl whom I adored jumped twice in one day, the second time because she said that if she didn't do it then, she never would. After that day, she never did, and her parents added jumping to a lengthening list of dangerous scrapes into which I had lured her. I took another girl out to Mansfield to ride in the back of the plane and watch me plummet from sight. When I plummeted, the pilot racked the plane onto its side so that she could see better and terrified the girl. She closed her eyes, hung on for dear life lest she fall out after me, and saw nothing.

"I jumped in several competitions, never so much as placing; I made several thirty-second delays, and had a close call.

"The close call was odd. It occurred on a twenty-second delay and set me back to tens for a while as a penalty for giving my jumpmaster an awful moment. I had plunged out in the normal manner, done the required barrel roll or loop or whatever I was supposed to be practicing, turned this way and that, and then as the bare autumn woods acquired resolution and the altimeter sped toward 2,500 feet—the altitude at which the movement of the ripcord pull was to be initiated—I reached in for the ripcord with my right hand and did not find it. What happened then is hard to explain. Rather than withdraw my hand, locate the ripcord with my eyes, and then reach for it again, I went on groping and falling, unable to see the handle because my hunting hand was in the way. I felt as though I had plenty of time, and this went on for six or seven seconds, until I finally found the D-ring and pulled. After the roar and snap of the opening, I found myself at about 1,100 feet—six or seven seconds of free fall from the ground. After I landed (in a backyard of a house in the woods, far from the DZ, and surrounded by yelling children) and found my way back, my jumpmaster wanted to know why I hadn't gone for my reserve the moment I failed to deploy the main chute. That was a tough one. I had felt no fear then, no sense of impending calamity in the trees which reached up with distinct branches to receive me. The reserve, I felt, was for clear-cut emergencies, not prolonged, uncounted seconds of incompetent fumbling. Some jumpers, I have heard, are thought to have fallen all the way to the ground in just such a search, paralyzed, I suppose, by the contrast between the insignificance of the problem and the imminence of the earth.

"Jumping has its lore, most of which deals with Death, who rides in the jump plane alongside you waiting to snap you up. It was said among us that there was a danger of something resembling rapture of the deep; the rising landscape might hypnotize the jumper and deprive him of his will to pull. There were spins which turned their victims into helpless pinwheels spread-eagled by centrifugal force. All the various kinds of malfunctions were neatly

To land on the right spot, the jumper works the parachute's risers to spill air from the chute. Body English also helps.

categorized and for each of them a rote emergency procedure had to be learned. There was the team of jumpers who had gone out on top of clouds, supposedly over land, but on emerging from the bottom of the overcast found themselves over the lake in which they were all destined to drown. There were stories of people who had survived malfunctions, such as a girl who had had a streamer—a chute which leaves the pack but doesn't blossom—in the Boston area and had fallen, her descent only slightly retarded by the drag of the trailing chute and her reserve unaccountably forgotten, into the shallow water of a lake. An old man and a child, seeing the bizarre accident, had gone out in a motorboat to fetch up the corpse, and had come back with a stunned but living passenger. There were paratroopers whose chutes had failed to open and who had fallen into trees or snow and lived; there were Russian troops trained to jump without chutes from low, slow planes; men who had jumped two with one chute, with varying degrees of reported success. There was a test pilot who had ejected from a dying jet and fallen into the only tree within miles, which happened to be in the front yard of a doctor's house who happened to be home, and whose neighbor was an ambulance driver who also happened to be home for lunch, with his ambulance.

"The backdrop of legend and fantasy distracted one's attention from the occasional and unromantic deaths, sickening falls and bounces unblessed by miraculous luck, which were blamed, as the inevitable casualties of dangerous popular pastimes always are, on some negligence or carelessness on the part of the deceased. Occasionally, someone died heroically. The serious, brown-haired one of my pair of early mentors stayed with a student who failed to pull until he got him to do so, and then he himself pulled, too late.

"In the face of the obvious risks, in the face of the hardly concealed thrill of repeatedly missing death by an inch rather than a mile, we blandly insisted that there was no danger if one were careful and sensible, and that we jumped for some reason other than to act out a mock suicide, or to impress ourselves and others with our coolness and courage.

"In the West, the discomforts, apart from death and the odd broken bone, were limited to sunburn, dust inhalation, and landings in cactus, one of which I made; in the East, there was throughout the bulk of the academic year the cold, which was bad enough on the ground and awesome at 120 miles an

The tensions of competition govern jumpers and judges alike.

hour at 10,000 feet. My jumpmaster's glasses had one lens which had spontaneously cracked when he had stepped out of the airplane into a Borean propblast. We wore incredible garments: a thermal union suit, quilted underwear, two pairs of pants and shirts, jackets, balaclavas, helmets, and goggles. We resembled participants in some Arctic expedition or Himalayan ascent, with barely a square centimeter of skin peeking out from among our insulations. We could hardly move, and had to be helped into the airplane and out of it with tugs and kicks, like armored knights hoisted with cranes onto their horses.

"The fall itself is unimaginable; its immediacy is such that one cannot piece together in fancy a satisfactory inkling of it. You spring backward from the step into empty space, so remote from the ground that it seems to exist in some other, unrelated sphere. The roar and blast of the prop cease momentarily; you see the airplane turn away, the jumpmaster's head disappearing in the doorway; you are weightless but it does not occur to you that you are. Rapidly you accelerate, or rather, you float isolated in the midst of an accelerating wind which in a few moments swells from a draft to a hurricane that roars in your ears, tears at your clothing, distorts your face into that of a gargoyle, lifts your goggles, and fills your eyes with tears. Your hands, shifting like delicate rudders, like a child's hand out a car window, turn you or stop your turning. Pulling in one arm and calf, you roll to that side; tucking in your head, you somersault. Lying on your back like a lounging swimmer looking into the sky, you are also like a lion tamer who turns away from his glowering beasts as you dare the altimeter to be wrong. Sweeping your arms back into a delta and slightly humping your back, you 'track,' picking up speed sharply and making good headway across the ground like some supersonic bomb, and then you pull your arms forward, straining with all your strength against the air, and lift your weight on your arms to slow down. You look at the ground coming up and try to *realize* it there, its lethal solidity, its genuineness, its bulk and detail. Altimeter, stopwatch: watch, watch, then stop, reach in across your chest for the chrome D and pull it firmly downward, keep it in your hand while you hear and feel (compressed into a second and a half) first the long stocking pulling up by the pilot chute and then the drag of the bag sliding up along the chute, the bustling nylon bubbling up and filling in a slow *whaaam!* as you snap down like the tip of a whip, and then, in sudden silence, sit on a swing half a mile high, alone with a light upward breath of breeze. You then slip the D-ring over your arm, catch hold of the wooden toggles that steer the chute, and begin methodically to maneuver toward your target.

"Hitting the ground is not like jumping from a particular height, 5 feet or 10 or 20 feet, because when you jump from a height your head and torso are still accelerating as they smack onto the ground, while in a parachute your upper body slows down as your weight is taken off the chute by your legs and

OPPOSITE. Staring intently at his aiming point, a jumper floats into the circle he has sought to invade from thousands of feet above.

butt hitting first, so that there is little chance of banging your head hard on the ground. Landing seemed curiously safe, though exciting; in nearly forty jumps, I hardly got a bruise, even coming down in stiff winds and being dragged along struggling with the so-called quick releases to unbuckle one set of risers and spill air from the chute, or landing in swampy water or in a tiny clearing in the woods or in rolling hummocky terrain. Drunk on air and plummeting, we were protected by the limberness of drunks.

"One had one's own chute, one's colors, one did one's own packing, one hung the heavy, sodden thing in one's room, which it nearly filled, to dry out after coming down in some midwinter, mid-Massachusetts morass. Mine was an antediluvian rig called a 5TU, meaning that it had two gores missing either five or seven gores apart on the back, with part of the bottom skirt in back missing, too, to give forward thrust. It came down hard and fast—21 feet per second, I was told—unlike the modern flower-like variations on the revolutionary Para-Commander, which I have seen ascend in thermals and which seems practically capable of cross-country flight.

"It now feels perfectly natural to step out of an airplane into empty space, and I doubt the old dread could return, at least not in its old force. Even at a remove of more than ten years, the experience of learning to jump remains in my mind with uncommon vividness. It's so bizarre, so one-pointed, so concentrated and free of idleness or distraction. To turn a primordial fear, the stuff of panicky dreams, into a sport is absurdly clever. I rationalized it at times as an education in dealing with fear. It was a partial education at best, though, since the fear was never allowed to reach the stage of stark terror. It was like standing close to the cage of an infuriated animal. Eventually, habit muffled one's instinctive avoidance of sheer drops and suicidal jumps, and one became a dilettante of mock suicides, jumping as indifferently from airplanes as from streetcars. Skydivers eventually become sportsmen like any others. The nature of the activity loses its poignancy, jumpers become absorbed in humdrum target practice and endless filming of grinning faces with vibrating cheeks or of slowly wheeling human stars. The beginning is the best—a trip into the unknown and dark interior of the soul where children's terrors dwell; the first few jumps take you where you want to go, the rest are practice."

SECTION TWO *Speed*

Introduction

ONE of the paradoxical sensations of flight is that of being suspended motionless in the air, or of moving with the slowness of an hour hand. It almost seems as though the faster an airplane is supposed to be, the slower it goes: from the window of a light airplane, the landscape is seen to creep by; from that of a jet airliner, it barely appears to move at all.

The reason is distance. The jet airliner is several miles up, and although it travels a mile every six seconds, those miles of distance above the ground make the landscape seem so small that the airplane seems barely to move. The light airplane, traveling perhaps 3 miles a minute but only a mile above the ground, appears to be the quicker of the two; an automobile going 30 miles an hour down a narrow lane seems fastest of all. If you wanted the ultimate sensation of speed, the answer might be an airplane flying down a narrow lane, which is very much like the sort of flying that air racing involves.

Speed has an odd fascination for many people. Some of them like speed in the abstract, the breaking of records apart from the personal sensations involved. Others are attracted to the sense of speed, to such sensations as the peripheral blur of the world hurtling by and the torrential roar of an engine near the point of explosion. Why is speed so appealing? Is it only that it overwhelms the senses, like a drug, focusing the mind and making distraction impossible? Is it the contrast between the power it implies and the helplessness of the individual human being, reflecting back to the times when a man's ability to run might be his only protection against danger?

The first air races were held in 1909 and produced speeds of around 40 miles an hour; this was considered breathtaking. The 1930s saw the speeds rise into the high 200s. After the war, racing planes pushed toward 400 miles per hour—500 in jet races—and lap speeds of over 400 miles an hour occur from time to time in present-day Unlimited racing.

Four hundred miles an hour, while flying only a wingspan above the ground. The stripped-down airframes do nothing to muffle or dampen the roar and vibration of the engines; the cockpits are hot and cramped under bubble canopies. In the Formula One ships, whose top speeds are in the 250s but whose tiny dimensions make the speed seem as great as that of the Unlimiteds, the scream of the over-revving engines rises and falls with the speed. Everything is a blur except for the expanding vista ahead and the vibrating instrument panel. Other racers bob about, sometimes looming suddenly above like a swooping hawk pouncing upon the space ahead. In a crowded turn, the air boils where many wings have plowed it, leaving invisible tornadoes like the roostertails that follow racing boats. Through the melee and the maelstrom the planes plunge, fierce and friendless, for minute after minute of interminable, burning concentration.

The straightaway is easy, the turns are terrible, and they come up every fifteen or twenty seconds. A checkered pylon seems to zoom toward the plane. As it comes close enough for the pilot to distinguish observers and photographers clustered around its foot, the pylon races up and overhead as the airplane banks sharply on edge, its stick hard back, the multiplied force of gravity pulling its pilot down—five Gs, six Gs, seven Gs—the blood leaving his head and the world going gray as he rolls out blind for a moment, flying by timing, waiting for sight to return and the next pylon to materialize ahead, hoping the sight is not preceded by the crash and tearing of a mid-air collision.

Air racing is the horizontal equivalent of free fall: a torrent of overwhelming sensations which the mind fixes with fiery concentration. Despite the dangers, collisions are rare, though when one occurs, death is almost inevitable. Engine failures and forced landings are frequent, with the airplanes, though not their pilots, frequent casualties. The crowds are more nostalgic and sympathetic than bloodthirsty. Many of the spectators are pilots and would-be pilots for whom the sight of a crash is more sickening than

exciting, evoking the image of one's self in the same situation with the same brief realization of helplessness and doom.

Race meetings occur infrequently; when they occur, fans come from all over the country to attend them. The fans buy pit passes to be able to walk among the old fighters, to crane at their huge propellers, or to peer, bending over, into the minuscule cockpits of the Formula Ones and biplanes. They huddle all day in a chilly autumn wind in the stands, munching hot dogs and drinking Cokes, waiting for the incomparable moment when somebody calls, "Here they come!" All eyes turn toward a string of specks descending from over the hills at 400 miles an hour heading for the moment when, as the roar of the engines swells from a faint murmur in the distance and the specks materialize into an echelon of fighters, the voice of renowned pilot and starter Bob Hoover crackles over the PA system as his P-51 pace plane pulls up and away: "Gentlemen, you have a race."

One of the earliest air meets. A Wright Flyer skims over the ground as it rounds a pylon. Pylons are used to mark closed aerial race courses of various shapes. Races have also been keyed to long-distance flying, some being transcontinental in scope.

CHAPTER

4. Air Racing

RACING could well be man's oldest sport. It seems to respond to an instinctive esteem for speed and to our natural impulse for competition. It is natural, then, that as men find ways to move faster, they are quick to turn the new forms of locomotion into vehicles of competition.

The first airplanes were very slow—skiers had probably already gone faster—but people must have appreciated the potential for improvement. It was plain that to go faster one had only to improve the aerodynamics and increase the power; hardly any finesse or luck was required beyond this. The first large-scale air race, the Rheims Meeting of 1909, was won by Glenn Curtiss, whose pusher biplane rounded the course at over 40 miles an hour. This was not an impressive speed, but the science of flight was still in its infancy. What *was* impressive was the rate at which improvements in designing were being made. Most designers were quick to appreciate the importance of streamlining—one did not have to go a long way from the principles of shipbuilding to see how airplanes must be shaped in order to sail through a sea of air—and by the end of the First World War, some remarkably clean and compact monoplanes and biplanes were capable of speeds of nearly 200 miles per hour. Airplanes became capable of speeds which had hitherto belonged only to projectiles. The races were on.

The performance gains of the 1920s and 1930s were phenomenal, both for land- and water-based planes. One of the most hotly contested prizes, for instance, was the Schneider Trophy for maximum speed in a seaplane. The seaplane configuration was inherently disadvantageous to fast flight since, in the majority of the competing airplanes, it required two enormous floats, each nearly as large as the fuselage. In spite of this gratuitous drag, the Schneider Trophy seaplanes were the fastest aircraft of their day. Their speeds were incredible. In 1933, an Italian Macchi-Castoldi seaplane set a record of nearly 441 miles per hour, which has stood—probably uncontested—ever since. For comparison, the record for all piston-engined aircraft, set in 1969, is 483 mph.

The remarkable progress in seaplane design was perhaps due mostly to the fact that the Schneider contest was among nations rather than among individuals. Entries were often financed by governments and air forces. One conspicuous exception was a wealthy British lady, who stepped into the breach when her government withdrew its support; she gave the astonishing sum of a hundred thousand pounds to the British team so that the Schneider Trophy could stay in England.

The U.S. government withdrew its participation from air racing after suffering an embarrassing defeat by a privately built racer in 1929. Landplane speeds in the Thompson Trophy races even in the late thirties barely exceeded 300 mph, perhaps because the private entrants could not afford the sort of engine research that went into the Schneider airplanes. They relied on airframe design for their advantages. The result was a larger variety of types than was found in the seaplane field, though some of the types, such as Steve Wittman's Bonzo, were highly specialized in conception and did not much influence the future design of high-speed aircraft. On the other hand, the liquid-cooled fighters of World War II were clear descendants of the later Schneider seaplanes. It is argued, in fact, that American air inferiority at the beginning of World War II was due to the failure of the U.S. government to take an active interest in air racing during the 1930s.

Air racing had a popularity in the thirties such as it will probably never approach again. Crowds numbered in the hundreds of thousands, and names like Roscoe Turner, Jacqueline Cochran, Steve Wittman, Bennie Howard, and Jimmie Doolittle were household words. Turner probably did more than anyone else to create the image of the scarf-and-goggles aviator. He was of stocky build, with an oversize smile and a waxed moustache; he always raced in jodhpurs and jodhpur boots, with a leather cap, goggles, and a military-

A Curtiss pusher, similar to that which won the Rheims air race in 1909.

looking jacket, so that he resembled Clark Gable trying out for the role of Benito Mussolini. Turner was a good sportsman with an unfortunate penchant for cutting pylons—a mistake which, according to the rules of the races at that time, required turning back immediately and making the pylon good. Turner once won a race only to be disqualified because he had circled a pylon one lap after cutting it, rather than turn back in the face of the field. Later, in the 1938 Thompson race, he cut a pylon, returned to circle it, and then, after being passed by the entire field, overtook them all in his Wedell-Williams Meteor and won the race.

There was a commitment among the early racers that no longer exists. They were professional racers and builders rather than hobbyists. The marked individuality of their machines reflected the character, inventiveness, and daring of the respective builders; the pilots often tested their airplanes as they competed in them. Thorough and systematic testing of aircraft is now taken for granted, but last-minute redesigns and engine changes were common in the thirties. Pilots and designers also showed a remarkable willingness to persevere with designs that had shown themselves to be vicious and unpredictable. Among these were the Granville Gee Bees.

The Gee Bees represented a fairly well-thought-out attempt to mount the largest conveniently available engine on the smallest airframe that could streamline the engine, carry a man and wings, and lift the whole ensemble. The first attempt, the Model Z, was slightly longer than a Volkswagen. It had a huge radial engine in front and a fuselage that tapered directly back from the cowling to the tail. Wind tunnel experiments indicated, however, that the thickness of the fuselage should increase behind the cowling—whence came the barrel-like profile of the more familiar R-1 and R-2 Bees, whose wings and tails appeared to have been swallowed up by a monstrously inflated fuselage.

The Model Z was destroyed, along with its pilot, when a fuel filler cap in front of the pilot came off, breaking the windshield. In his attempt to pull up to make altitude for a forced landing, the pilot broke a wing spar. Later Gee Bees had controllability problems, and in a couple of cases swerved from the runway and then, after becoming airborne over the heads of an alarmed crowd, went into uncontrollable rolls and crashed. Various others came to similarly unfortunate ends, their problems sometimes aggravated by attempts to replace the original 535-hp Pratt & Whitney Wasp engine with others of up to 800 horsepower. So large an engine driving a front-mounted propeller could hardly help producing a powerful flow field around the tiny airplane, immersing its wings and tail in a rotating wash with which they could not always cope. The designers had been optimistic about the effectiveness of the tiny control surfaces; the R-1 Gee Bee, in fact, first emerged from the factory with no vertical tail at all, the broad back end of the airplane having been considered sufficient guarantee of directional stability. When the plane proved violently unstable, a small fin was added above the turtledeck, and the rudder area was much increased, rendering the airplane just manageable.

By comparison, the Wedell-Williams racer of Roscoe Turner, which eventually carried engines of 1,000 hp, was conventional in layout, with sufficient wingspan and tail area to provide good handling characteristics. Its flying qualities were, in fact, exceptional, and in the end it was probably the most successful racer of its day. At the opposite extreme from the Gee Bee, Steve Wittman's homemade Bonzo had broad, stubby wings and an extremely long and slender fuselage with tail surfaces of normal proportions, so that it, like the Wedell-Williams, flew well. The moral of the story, it seemed, was that extremes should be avoided, and that what flew best ultimately raced best.

By the late thirties, the terrible loss of life among the racing fraternity had brought home the necessity of more thorough programs of testing and maintenance. It was too late, however, to put the lesson to much use. The last Thompson Trophy race was flown in 1939 and was won by the aging Roscoe Turner, who then announced his retirement from racing. The 1939 races were the last held until after the Second World War.

During the war, aerodynamic research fell almost exclusively into the hands of the National Advisory Committee for Aeronautics (NACA, later to become NASA) and the aircraft companies—Bell, North American, United Aircraft, Grumman, Curtiss, and so on—that built fighter and bomber aircraft. The size and reliability of the engines increased, new types of airfoils were experimented with, and the conditions for getting the maximum performance out of an airplane came to be better understood. By the end of the war, radial engines of over 3,000 horsepower were driving 7-ton fighters at over 400 miles an hour. Jets had just begun to appear, capable of speeds of nearly 600 miles an hour. Breaking the sound barrier was near, and propeller-driven airplanes had reached the theoretical limits of their performance (because of losses in prop efficiency when parts of the propeller go supersonic). Air racing resumed in 1946 at Cleveland; the participating planes were all ex-fighters, some of them heavily modified; the excitement was high. There were races for jets as well as for props, and also for the small homebuilts, which eventually came to be called Formula Ones. It seemed as though air racing was well reestablished as a national sport, until a Mustang went out of control at Cleveland and crashed into a backyard, killing a woman and her baby. Quite suddenly, big-time air racing came to an end.

Racing was revived by an ex-racer named Bill Stead at his ranch near Reno, Nevada, in 1964. A number of pilots owning ex-World War II fighters

OPPOSITE. Action at the 1949 Goodyear air races at Cleveland. The pusher plane (top) was unusual. ABOVE. What were called "midget" racers in 1949 lined up at the Goodyear event to await qualifying heats.

showed up to have a look, not seriously imagining that they would be competitive, because, so they thought, the old pros would be back. But the old pros weren't back; and so the tyros went at it, learning from scratch what pylon racing was all about. Some of them were fierce competitors, and the races, supported by their encouragement and their ready cash, thrived. They took place in the following years at the decommissioned Stead Air Force Base, also near Reno, with races for Unlimiteds, Formula Ones, Sport Biplanes, Stock Planes, and an AT-6 class created, presumably, because there were so many AT-6s. around to fill it. Besides the annual Reno meet, there were somewhat less reliable races at Cleveland, Cape May, Lancaster and Mojave, California, Las Vegas, Fort Lauderdale, and elsewhere. Recently, only the most vigorous meets—Reno and the popular, easily organized Mojave

Unlimited racing has helped keep interest in World War II airplanes, such as this P-51, alive.

1,000—have taken place regularly, but the racing community does its best to support every new attempt to arrange a racing event.

The principal classes today begin with the Unlimiteds, all of them ex-fighters or bombers with piston engines. Turbine engines are not allowed, but otherwise there is no limitation on the contestants, and a few of the airplanes have been heavily modified—most notably, the monotonously victorious Grumman Bearcat of a former Lockheed test pilot, Darryl Greenamyer. Unlimiteds are expensive to buy and fly, and most of the participants are prosperous airline pilots, car dealers, doctors, or the like. Lap speeds are usually around 400 mph on an 8-mile course. A few Corsairs, P-38s and P-39s, Douglas B-26s, and Hawker Sea Furies have participated in Unlimited racing, but the bulk of the competitors are P-51 Mustangs and Grumman Bearcats with their engines tweaked, their seams sealed, and their wings clipped.

The purple P-51 of Clay Lacy, an air race star.

The Unlimiteds, in addition to appearing in closed-course pylon races, had, until a few years ago, a transcontinental event sponsored by Harrah's Club in Reno, modeled after the old Bendix Trophy Race which started from what is now Hollywood-Burbank Airport in Los Angeles and ended in Cleveland. In the thirties, large crowds came even in the middle of the night to see the Bendix racers leave; but in the sixties, their departure from Milwaukee was unattended by much public interest, and their arrival in Reno noted principally by the timers. The transcontinental race was finally abandoned, to be replaced in spirit at least by the Mojave 1,000, a distance event held annually around a long, closed course at Mojave, California.

The requirements for long-distance racers are somewhat different from those for pylon racers, principally in the matter of range, but also in that of engine reliability. Back in the days of the Bendix, when the fastest pylon racers had to stop for fuel two or three times between Los Angeles and Cleveland, a

A racing Douglas B-26 (not to be confused with the Martin B-26 Marauder). Multi-engine planes seldom race, except for the Lockheed P-38, which was designed as a fighter. The B-26 served in World War II and Korea as an attack bomber.

winning stratagem was to have a slower airplane with the range to make the trip nonstop, or with only one stop; this was the method employed by Bennie Howard in his remarkable comparatively small-engined *Mister Mulligan* in the 1935 Bendix, which he won by a twenty-three-second margin over Roscoe Turner.

Part of the lack of interest in the modern transcontinental race probably stemmed from the fact that any passenger liner now crossed the country in less time than the fastest racer, and so there seemed to be nothing remarkable in the performance of the Mustangs and Bearcats flying, out of sight of everyone, between Milwaukee and Reno. In the thirties, records for transcontinental flights had been repeatedly set and broken by the same airplanes that flew in the Bendix and Thompson races.

Before the transcontinental events disappeared, a few planes had been specially equipped for them, notably a wet-wing Mustang belonging to the

An AT-6 rounding the corner, powerful, fast, and loud.

Banking hard into a tight turn, a sport biplane.

Lined up and revving to go, a heat of racing biplanes.

late E. D. Wiener, and Darryl Greenamyer's Bearcat "Conquest I." Neither airplane achieved anything noteworthy in long-range racing, however, and both are now retired from action.

The next class in size, if not in speed, is the AT-6. The "T-6," known in the Navy as the SNJ and in England as the Harvard, was the main Army Air Force advanced trainer in World War II; it was nicknamed "Texan." A well-prepared T-6 turns in lap speeds of about 200 mph. Dozens of them turn up every year to race, and they make a crowded, colorful, and noisy, if rather ungainly, spectacle as they motor around the pylons, making up in nearness to the ground what they lack in speed.

Like the T-6s, the Sport Biplanes depend for competitive interest on the limitations of the class. Two wings are slower than one, and only lately have the slickest all-metal biplanes with their 290-cubic-inch engines of 125 stock horsepower attained speeds of over 200 mph. The Sport Biplane class is in a way the most attractive one to a new entrant, however, because its possibilities have been least exploited. Most of the competitors run highly modified stock midget biplanes whose original purpose was fun flying and aerobatics. They are not aerodynamically clean and they achieve their performance in spite of many rather obvious disadvantages. In the last couple of years, a few exquisitely sleek metal and fiberglass ships have appeared and have kept the promise of their looks with record speeds. Despite the inherent drawbacks of the biplane configuration, the class is now achieving speeds equal to those of the inherently cleaner Formula Ones of ten years ago.

The Formula One class calls for a monoplane wing of 66 square feet, two fixed wheels, a stock 100-hp Continental engine, and a moderately reclined pilot position. Except for the fixed landing gear, there is nothing inherently draggy in the specification, and such racers are now reaching speeds of nearly 270 mph on the straightaway. Their lap speeds on the 3-mile course are about 225 mph, showing the importance of cornering speed. Less radical design has been done in Formula One than in Sport Biplane, curiously, even though the potential speeds are higher, perhaps because there is so much more room for improvement and, therefore, more chance of paying for one's efforts with victories and prizes, in the biplanes. The Formula One specification is really just a description of a small, fast airplane; it sets up few artificial barriers to speed, and Formula One racers were consequently fast from the beginning; not very much can be done to improve them. The only radically new attempt is a fiberglass pusher model with a shrouded propeller; but its performance is not much different from that of the average Formula One, and it seems to have been designed more for looks than for peak efficiency.

Stock plane racing, which was traditionally reserved for women by a community that will probably be among the last ever to have its consciousness "raised," is now rarely seen; for a Formula Vee class, using Volkswagen engines in an attempt to keep the cost of construction within the reach of competitors, has not yet achieved sufficient numbers to appear in the major races.

People go to the air races for various reasons. Some are aficionados of certain classes of planes, although it is generally agreed that the majority of the

A Formula One racer, part of an increasingly popular class.

Ray Cote's Shoestring, a winning plane. According to Cote, "We painted it sky blue so they wouldn't see us coming. Turned out, it wasn't necessary."

spectators get the greatest thrill from the Unlimiteds. Some are just airplane fans, who would go a long way to see anything fly, especially if it's a bit noisier, faster, and more powerful than the run-of-the-mill plane. At Reno, the races are mingled with a continuous air show, since the logistics of getting airplanes into and out of the air safely make each race a small island of action surrounded by a sea of preparations and moppings up. Aerobatic acts fill the gaps between heats, and for an additional entry fee, the spectator can gain admission to the "pits," that part of the ramp where the competing airplanes are parked, and walk among the towering propellers of the Unlimiteds or peer into the tiny cockpits of the Formula Ones. Just a meditative look at the pigeonhole into which a Formula pilot squeezes himself to fly around the pylons does much to convey a sense of the intensity of the piloting experience.

Part of the appeal of the Unlimiteds is in their historic evocations; part is their sheer hurtling power, the union of the force of a locomotive with the bulk of an automobile; like big dragsters, the Unlimited racers have the quality of an explosion in harness. Since the class is Unlimited, it has drawn some comical contenders, like Clay Lacy's entry of a four-engine airliner in the Mojave 1,000. But its big hope lies in the custom racers not yet built. There has been talk for years about the possibilities: airplanes hardly larger than a Formula One hitched to the giant engine of a fighter; or stripped-down fighters with two or three times the power originally installed. Drawings crop up from time to time in magazines: for instance, a twin-boom arrangement with a central fuselage pod containing two Allison engines of 1,200 stock horsepower each, one pushing, one pulling, with the pilot nestled uncomfortably between them. Wings are almost an afterthought. There is much talk of automotive engines. Offenhausers (which combine small size, high power, and the reliability required for long events like the Indianapolis 500) and Donovans (which are said to provide dragsters with 2,000 hp for short spurts) might drive a pusher flying wing at 450 mph, with a nearly supine pilot, leading with his feet, shoehorned into a lean fiberglass and Plexiglas pod like a sailplane's.

Unhappily, the costs of developing such airplanes these days are great, and the risks to the pilots greater still. The combination of a large engine with

Most of the activity in an air race is that of the ground crews slaving to keep engines at peak condition.

a small airframe can be unmanageable, as was made obvious by some of the racers of the thirties; but then, at least, the track was being beaten into the unknown and deaths could be rationalized on the ground that these were pioneers and that not all could expect to reap only the benefits of such work. Now, the work has been done; it is glory alone that tempts people to dream of custom racers.

Like everything these days at which large numbers of people may be expected to congregate, air racing is heavily commercialized. It is not a participation sport, but a spectator sport. There are many sorts of races—the so-called proficiency races, for instance—in which any pilot may participate, and these are more in the spirit of sport flying than are the big spectator events. The fact that big races exist, though, robs the little races of their appeal. However much fun a dozen pilots may have in setting off on a 300-mile course against a clock and a handicap, they must always feel insignificant because they are flying Cessnas, not Mustangs and Bearcats. Similarly, even the Formula One and Sport Biplane pilots, however intense their competition and monumental their efforts to refine their airplanes, have an uphill fight against the sheer might and impressiveness of the Unlimiteds.

The modern pylon races are nearly as dangerous as their prewar counterparts, because if the airplanes are more reliable, the pilots are probably less so. In the twenties and thirties, minor races were held constantly, and there seemed to be an uninterrupted flow of prize money from many sources. Now races are rare and many of the participants are relatively inexperienced. Mid-air collisions are frequent, and several deaths have resulted from failure to escape from a burning or disabled aircraft.

Formula One great Bob Downey and his plane *Old Tiger.*

Air racing will never again be as democratic as it was in the beginning, and as it can still be, wherever just a few pilots get together for a friendly contest. Nor will it ever again advance with the intensity it had in the thirties, when each new refinement broke new ground. The Second World War was perhaps the turning point; after it, everything that could be done to gain speed had been done, the racers were no longer the fastest airplanes in the world, the records were out of reach of a pylon course, and the peculiar vitality of the twenties and thirties had been extinguished.

But then a horse is a horse, and people still go to horse races. The tone of air racing may have changed, but the nostalgia, excitement, and danger are still there, and people still respond to them. Reno has its cold winds, but no one notices the chill when, between the barks of the PA system, you hear from down in the pits the cough of an engine starting, and look that way to see, over the heads of people and over the tops of the airplanes, a towering windmill starting to turn, the puffs of white smoke, the sudden blur and the roar as the huge engine catches, stumbles, and then grows deep and smooth as a river.

The chief thrill about Formula One racing is that of maneuvering well in tight formations and gaining the advantage.

You watch the half-visible disk of the whirling prop, see it move out and swing around followed by the top of a fin and rudder that tell what kind of airplane, and whose, it is; watch them creep toward you as the crowd parts, while to either side, first singly and then in small groups, other props start to turn and other smoke signals rise and flee on the vibrating air. One engine, two, three, a chorus now are singing in their basses and baritones, and they come to you in a line, Indian file, sashaying right and left as the pilots crane first from one side of the cockpit, then the other. The moment is timeless and electric; it is as though so many mammoths or mastodons were deliberately emerging from some ancient bog before an enchanted traveler, seeming both strange and familiar, terrifying and soothing at once. As long as these props that once turned in anger turn again in pride and challenge, there will be people who will come from far away and feel privileged to see them.

CHAPTER **5.** *The Making of Conquest I*

On August 16, 1969, the world speed record held since April 1939 by a Messerschmitt Me-209R fell to Darryl Greenamyer's modified Grumman Bearcat, Conquest I. One month later, the airplane was retired after winning its fifth successive Reno Unlimited race. Having dominated air racing for five years, to the point that many of Greenamyer's competitors did not even bother to try to catch him, Conquest I had apparently reached the end of the road.

A long and costly road it had been. When the late Bill Stead revived air racing at Reno in 1964, the plane was there, unpainted, lightly modified, with race number I—just a coincidence, since it was available and easy to paint—and the lucky registration number of N1111L. Greenamyer, an inveterate racer, had bought an interest in the plane in June of 1964 from two doctors in Antelope Valley, California. With only three months to go before the projected races, Greenamyer and his merry men had set out to make a racer of the stock F8F-2 Bearcat.

Each of the crew was a specialist who contributed his know-how to the effort gratis: Ray Poe, a Lockheed flight engineer, was crew chief; with him were Cecil McMain and Randy Scoville, mechanics; Ron Waagmeester, pilot; Pete Law and Bruce Boland, Lockheed thermodynamics and structures engineers, respectively; "social director" Bob Flaherty; and an aeronautics student, Bill Kerchenfaut.

86

Conquest I, Darryl Greenamyer's recast Grumman F8F-2 Bearcat.

The F8F was a small, light naval fighter designed in 1943 as a replacement for the F6F Hellcat. Intended to operate even from small carriers and to exceed the Hellcat in climb and maneuverability, the original F8F-1 had a 35-foot, 10-inch wingspan, a Pratt & Whitney R-2800-22W engine rated at 2,100 hp for takeoff, and a gross weight of less than 8,800 pounds. Production Bearcats were fitted with the -34W version of the 2800 engine; on the F8F-2, this was changed to a -30W engine, rated at 2,300 hp for takeoff. The -2 Bearcat was similar to the -1 in appearance, differing only in a modified cowling and vertical tail, armament, and armor. The -2 version appeared in 1948, and deliveries were completed in May 1949. In all, 1,263 Bearcats were delivered. The top speeds of the stock F8F-2, with its gross weight of 10,426 pounds, were 447 mph at 28,000 feet and 387 mph at sea level. It landed at 105 mph, climbed at 4,420 feet per minute, and had a ceiling of 40,700 feet.

The armor and armament had already been removed from N1111L. Greenamyer's team now removed the large, stock bubble canopy and replaced it with a much smaller one scrounged together out of odd parts—some of them from a P3A.

The original 185-gallon bag-type fuselage fuel tank (located between

The square-wing Conquest always attracted crowds, as if it were a monument to speed.

the front and rear wing spars beneath the pilot) was removed, and the entire compartment was caulked with integral tank sealant, bringing its capacity up to 310 gallons. (Part of the wing was sealed as well, with the intention of flying the plane in a transcontinental race, but this plan was never carried out.)

Unpainted, except for numbers and a Goldwater-spectacled elephant's head on the cowling, the plane went to Reno. The races were held in 1964 at the small Sky Ranch Airport, not at Stead Air Force Base, where they have been ever since. The runway surface was rough and unsuitable for the narrow high-pressure tires on the Bearcat. After winning the first qualifying heat, Greenamyer decided not to land back at Sky Ranch, and went to Reno Municipal instead; in consequence, he was disqualified. (He had been afraid of nosing over, since his airplane was nose-heavy from the removal of the radio and radar equipment originally placed behind the pilot.) So he left Reno with the airplane, but nothing else.

The bulk of the modifications to the plane were done between the 1964

The hugeness of the plane was mainly to house an enormous powerplant.

and 1965 Reno races. Over 3,000 man-hours went into the job in that year alone, as well as a good fraction of the hundred thousand dollars that Greenamyer estimates the Bearcat has cost.

First, the wings were clipped. This was an easy job, since the F8F was equipped with breakaway wing tips. A 42-inch outer panel of each wing was separately skinned and held to the inner portion of the wing, with bolts designed to fail at a load lower than that at which the inner section of the main spar would fail. If the pilot pulled excessive G-loads in combat, the outer wing panels would separate, protecting the inner wing from failure. Straps had been installed to cover the breakaway seam in the skin; these were detached, the bolts undone and the wing tips removed, reducing the span to about 27.5 feet. Special racing wing tips were designed by Mel Cassidy, a Lockheed aerodynamicist, and fabricated in sheet aluminum.

The original Bearcat was equipped with a slotted flap of fabric and metal construction, with hinges protruding below the lower surface of each wing. These flap hinges were removed, the fabric skins were stripped off, and the sheet-metal covering of the wing was extended continuously to the trailing edge.

The crude bubble canopy was replaced with a tiny, smooth, Formula One canopy of molded Plexiglas, in which there was barely room for Greenamyer's head to turn from side to side. The integral fuselage tank, which had developed leaks because of relative movement of its parts under flight loads, was resealed. An external strap, running most of the length of the underside of the main spar and protruding about a quarter of an inch, was faired with balsa wood and body putty.

The entire electrical system was removed from the aircraft. All its instruments were direct-reading, and a 15-volt dry-cell battery was carried in the cockpit to power the gear warning lights and radio. The engine was started with ground power controlled by an external switch panel, which was disconnected once the engine was running. The electric auxiliary fuel pump was replaced with a hand wobble pump.

The hydraulic system also went; only the main cylinders on the landing gear were retained, and a small (about 5 inches in diameter and 20 inches long) nitrogen bottle was installed to activate the gear. Charged with nitrogen at 1,900 psi, the bottle was good for one raising of the gear. Gravity was used to lower it. The gear was made to retract very rapidly—in less than five seconds—because it was thought that the Unlimited races might use a race-car start, but this proved not to be the case.

The wing root leading-edge air intakes for the oil cooler and carburetor were sealed up with sheet-metal fairings. In order to eliminate the aerodynamic drag of the oil cooler, it was immersed in a 24-inch boiler filled with the ADI (anti-detonant injection) mixture of alcohol and water, which was fed into the cylinders at manifold pressures exceeding 50 inches. This boiler, which was to undergo a number of modifications and relocations in the development of the airplane, was originally placed ahead of the firewall and vented through a small hole in front of the cockpit on the left side of the fuselage. The boiler, with a capacity of 7 to 10 gallons, boiled off about 35 of the 60 to 75 gallons of ADI used by the airplane in a race. (The use of a water boiler for oil cooling had been one of the modifications incorporated in the Me-209R that had bettered 469 mph in 1939.)

The -30W engine was replaced with an R-2800-83A, with a takeoff rating of 2,100 hp. In place of the updraft carburetor of the -30W, the -83A was equipped with a downdraft carburetor. An intake duct was constructed to run up behind the engine and over the rear row of cylinders; it opened between the front and rear cylinder rows, and breathed air from under the cowling that had passed over the top of the first row. The cowl flaps, located on the upper rear edge of the cowling, were bolted in the shut position, leaving only a small slot for the release of cooling air.

The stock F8F prop was replaced with one from a Douglas AD-1 Skyraider; this one had a diameter of 13 feet 6 inches and weighed 425 pounds. Since this prop was some 11 inches larger than the stock one, and the Bearcat was rather critical in prop clearance to start with, N1111L had to be taken off and landed in the three-point position. In a level attitude, the prop would have hit the ground. The engine nose was replaced with an R-2800-44 type—a low prop-speed gearing with a prop/crankshaft ratio of .35:1, giving a prop speed of 980 rpm at normal engine speed of 2,800 rpm, and a tip speed of nearly 700 mph at 400 knots.

Originally spinnerless, the plane was fitted with a spinner from a P-51H Mustang. At the other end, the blunt tip of the tail cone from which the arrester hook had extended was faired over with what looked like a pointed stinger. The stinger was later knocked off when the plane jumped its chocks and broke a tie-down chain during a full-power run-up. A new stinger with a sharp, straight upper edge was installed in its place.

Thus modified, the 'Cat went to Reno (still unpainted and with the Goldwater emblem removed from the nose) and won. Later, it qualified at Las Vegas with a speed of 424 mph.

In the spring of 1966, a new boiler was made, containing two oil coolers in place of one, and was installed in the lower part of the fuselage behind the cockpit. A new breather port was placed in the upper left side of the fuselage, behind the cockpit. The integral fuel tank, which was leaking again, was resealed.

Stainless steel slippers were installed on the upper and lower surfaces of the horizontal tail to close the elevator gaps, and the aileron gaps were sealed with Ceconite. In an attempt (that later proved ill-advised) to reduce the wetted area, the upper 18 inches of the vertical tail were clipped off.

The -83 supercharger was replaced with a CB-17 type (used on the DC-6, Convair, and other multi-engined craft), boosting the maximum power to 2,500 hp—at some expense in reliability, however, because the power section was still the less beefy -83A type. A low-tension ignition system was installed. An after-spinner fairing from a Constellation was inserted behind the propeller, covering the engine nose case and the inner lips of the cowling, which simply stopped in a smooth contour over the cylinders.

At this point, the Smirnoff Vodka firm offered sponsorship to Greenamyer, and the plane was at last painted—white with blunt-nosed blue arrows on the fuselage and wings. With painting, the entire skin was filled and smoothed, and the elevator gap seals—which had proved to impair longitudinal stability—were removed.

Conquest I, wearing its Smirnoff identification, lined up with rival Unlimiteds and tiny Formula Ones.

At the 1966 Los Angeles Air Races at Lancaster, California, Greenamyer made his first assault on the piston speed record. The stubby, avocado-shaped Bearcat, deprived of much of its vertical tail's area and aspect ratio, tried to fly sideways if Greenamyer took his feet off the rudder pedals. The speed record attempt was abandoned. Having borrowed a stock tail assembly from Bill Fornof, the owner of a familiar copper-and-black unmodified Bearcat, Greenamyer won Reno '66 with his usual ease.

The plane was returned to Las Vegas, its customary wintering place. The endlessly leaking integral tank was again resealed, and the oil-cooler boiler modified and its position changed slightly. Equipment for the injection of nitromethane and water was installed. Still sponsored by Smirnoff and otherwise unaltered from 1966, the plane won the 1967 Reno Unlimited Pylon Race.

It remained parked in Reno, during the winter, in a hangar. At one point, for some reason, it was removed from the hangar, and stood outside through a sandstorm. Greenamyer's crew arrived to find the plane full of sand, the canopy scarred and pitted, and the engine much in need of service. They installed a spare canopy, sending the sandblasted one back to its fabricator for polishing. The plane was cleaned up, and a small trailing-edge fairing was installed at the wing root to smooth out the airflow, which the black exhaust track on the side of the fuselage had revealed to be oscillating widely up and down on its way to the tail.

The integral tank was resealed, the fairing on the underwing strap was smoothed, and the entire airplane was repainted—this time all white. Greenamyer flew the plane from Las Vegas to Edwards Air Force Base in August 1968 for another attempt at the world speed record.

En route, the newly installed cockpit canopy split along the side, and its after-edge rose several inches upwards; the crack stopped, however, sparing Greenamyer the inconvenience of having his head scooped off as the canopy departed backwards. At Edwards, the broken canopy was replaced with the original one, which had been polished back to transparency by its maker, and the plane was ready for the record.

No luck. During a preparatory run at 500 mph, a piston blew—probably because of sand damage. The piston and cylinder were replaced the following week; but then the rebuilt engine seized during warmup, and was ruined.

Greenamyer then borrowed an R-2800 CA-18 engine from Aircraft Cylinder, Inc., a Sun Valley, California, engine-maintenance firm. Using the same -44 nose case and Skyraider prop, and essentially the same supercharger as the -83A engine, he went to Reno and again won—this time running only 2 mph faster than Chuck Hall, whose P-51 Mustang turned an unusually high 386 mph on the final heat.

Conquest I was returned to Vegas for the winter.

Bill Fornof wanted his tail back. Greenamyer's crew accordingly spent the winter building up the old vertical tail to its original height and installing an enlarged dorsal fin, after consultations with Grumman (which they doubtless wished they had had prior to making the original modification).

The integral fuel tank had lately deteriorated to such a point that it had been necessary to fill the water and gasoline tanks (separated only by a bulkhead) simultaneously, to prevent a bubbly head of either liquid developing and aggravating the leakage from one tank to the other. It was necessary to drain the Bearcat's sump just before each takeoff as a precaution against excessive fuel contamination. At last, they constructed three welded aluminum tanks and installed them in the fuselage compartment; thereafter, there was no trouble with fuel leakage.

Greenamyer acquired pistons and cylinders of the CB-17 type and installed them in the CA-18 crankcase from the borrowed engine; to this power section, he attached the overhauled blower from the old engine—a CB-17 type to start with—and the old -44 nose section. He now (in July 1969) had a complete CB-17 engine, with the exception of the -83 crankcase; that is, he had CB-17 power plus airliner reliability.

Back at Edwards for a new speed record attempt, the landing gear doors that previously had been opening a half inch or so at high speeds (because of the pressure difference between the outside and inside of the wing) were fitted with backward-facing airscoops to vent the overpressure.

Grumman was again consulted on the subject of the exhaust blast,

The sight of the white Bearcat leading the pack became commonplace to the point of monotony.

which was directed outward from the fuselage, leaving a stain over a wide area of the wing trailing edge. In order to narrow the exhaust wake, extensions lying flat against the sides of the fuselage were added to the exhaust pipes, and a cuff was installed to cover the exhaust roots where they emerged from beneath the cowling. After a test flight, it was apparent that the fuselage sides might suffer from exposure to the 600-degree exhaust, and a stainless steel shield 5 feet long was riveted to the fuselage side along the exhaust path. Behind it, however, the white paint was blistered all the way to the tail.

On August 16, the airplane as it then stood was flown four times along Edwards's 3-kilometer course—with appropriate official timers—and the world record speed of 483.041 mph was established. On his best run, Greenamyer was indicating about 510 mph, turning 3,000 rpm, and pulling 75 inches with nitromethane injection.

During this record flight, Greenamyer was subjected to cockpit temperatures of about 200 degrees, and he suffered burns on his hands, traced to exhaust leaks from a coupling beneath the cowling; hot exhaust was flowing out of the cowl-flap slots and into the small ventilating louvers on the canopy frame. Exhaust stains were actually found on the inside of the frame. The cause of the exhaust leak was the increased exhaust back pressure caused by the extensions; since nothing could be done about it, Greenamyer strapped an icepack to his chest on which to cool his hands while flying. The cockpit had never been a hospitable place to start with; ram effect alone raised the temperature of the 100-degree desert air to 140 degrees as it entered the cockpit, and the air was also full of fumes, which unaccountably found their way into the cockpit from the oil-cooler boiler. Greenamyer breathed through an oxygen mask while flying the airplane.

From Edwards, Conquest I went to Reno, qualified at 414 mph, and effortlessly won the Unlimited finals, at 412 mph—15 mph above the long-standing record for Unlimited competitive heats that had been set by Cook Cleland in a clipped-wing Corsair at Cleveland in 1949.

That was to be the end of Conquest I's career; it now was donated to the Fighter Aircraft Museum—which took over its sponsorship from Smirnoff, and of which Greenamyer is the founding father. Up to this point, the career of Conquest I had been one of consistent, almost routine success from the first; but the ease with which the airplane piled win upon win was the result of tireless work, massive expense, and a great deal of professional knowledge and ingenuity. In its final form, Conquest I was a tall, flat, stub-winged airplane with an empty weight of 5,800 pounds, of which 2,300 pounds was the big DC-6 engine. Its power loading in racing trim was less than 3 pounds per horsepower; its fuel consumption at full power was on the order of 300 gallons per hour. The instrumentation was quite normal, with the addition of a torque pressure gauge reading horsepower directly in the form of oil pressure. During his record run, Greenamyer read 3,200 hp; in racing, he confined himself to 2,800 rpm for his winning speed of 412 mph at Reno in 1969. Greenamyer attributed his success to his strategy of modifying his airframe for minimum drag, while keeping his engine more or less stock—unlike the majority of other racers, who run highly tweaked engines in stock or nearly stock airframes. The takeoff power rating of the CB-17 engine in the DC-6, he points out, is only 3 inches lower than that which he used at Reno, with the same rpm.

The combined modifications to powerplant and airframe that Green-amyer and his crew made between 1964 and 1969 netted them a speed increase of nearly 100 knots over the stock Bearcat in combat configuration—of which 40 or 50 knots came from the 1965 aerodynamic cleanup alone. (It is important to realize that while Greenamyer's record speed of 483 mph may not seem extraordinary compared with the 507 mph, for instance, with which the XP-47J is credited, it was achieved at low altitude; the maximum speeds normally cited for piston-engined fighter types are for high-altitude flight, and their sea-level top speeds are usually in the neighborhood of 350 mph.)

Like many who come to Reno, Greenamyer should have stopped while he was ahead. By his account, he retired the airplane in 1969 because he felt that its monotonous winning streak had a depressing effect upon air racing and prevented fresh blood from entering the sport. This sounded like a noble reason. At some point between the Septembers of 1969 and 1970, however, the noble spirit deserted Greenamyer, and he turned up again to race. Luck now deserted him as well. The nitrogen-powered landing gear, which his crew

Rival pilot Chuck Lyford well knew the frustrations of challenging Conquest I. Here, his crew mourns the death of yet another engine, blown in Lyford's P-51 during a race against the Bearcat.

had watched anxiously through the years in apprehension of its failing at some critical moment, failed. In a dramatic but unfortunately improper proceeding, Greenamyer landed, got his nitrogen bottle almost instantly recharged, and took off again just as the starting lineup was diving toward the first straightaway and in defiance of Bob Hoover's messages to remain on the ground. The gear still would not retract fully; like a crippled heron, Conquest I flew a grindingly slow, hopeless race with the half-folded strut dangling from its right wing.

Greenamyer returned with the plane in 1971 and won, but was fined for flying over the stands. Later that season, in consequence of an unsavory incident at the Mojave 1,000 Mile Race, the FAA removed Greenamyer's pilot's license and the Professional Race Pilot's Association suspended him for a period, which included the next Reno races. The airplane appeared at Reno in 1972, however, piloted by a friend of Greenamyer's who flew with the same flawless precision as Greenamyer but was disqualified for flying too low.

In the meantime, litigation had raised its ugly head. Dr. Phil Cousins, one of the original owners of the Bearcat, sued Greenamyer on the grounds that the original agreement had called for Greenamyer to maintain and occasionally race the airplane, but that in fact neither of the two original owners had ever gotten to fly it after Greenamyer entered the partnership, and the race modifications had made the plane unflyable for Cousins, who was of much larger physical stature than Greenamyer. The court found in Cousins's favor; the upshot was the forced sale of the airplane and partition of the proceeds.

For a while, the airplane that set the world's speed record for piston-engine planes sat silent and wind-beaten, like Bodhidharma facing the wall, beside a hangar at Mojave Airport. Its only companion was a legless, armless, equally mute AT-6. They were a sobering sight—a fighter and a trainer who didn't know when to leave the ring. But Conquest I and Greenamyer are of stiffer stuff than to allow that sad condition to last. By 1975, Conquest I was racing again at Mojave, wearing the American Jet Industries logo on its fuselage and with Greenamyer in its cockpit.

SECTION THREE *Escape*

Introduction

A CHILD looks up from his play and in a dreamy moment sees in the sky a white, straight trail and at its head, unimaginably far away, a triangular glint. He strains to hear the sound of the jet engines he knows are there, but the thing is so far away, so minute, that its sound is swallowed up in the blue immensity of the sky.

Men in airplanes, like men in submarines and men in moonships, are remote and isolated from the world. They may not feel alone, and they may talk and act as if they were in a normal, everyday place, but in doing so, they are losing one of the central and poignant experiences of flight, the sense of aloneness, of escape into themselves.

Every pilot knows such solitude. He has met it when he has forgotten, for a second, to shut out the disorienting vastness of the sky, the unreal and disconnected quality of the flat and distant earth and the paradoxical impression of hardly moving, when he knows he must be moving very, very fast. It is a solitude wed to fear, and those who do not want to be visited by the grimmer guest usually exclude both. But pilots who have come to terms with the existential shocks of altitude and isolation have found in the solitude of flight a sweet escape; it erases their cares, calms their hearts, gives them a taste of a godlike kind of suspension of self.

A Chinese story tells how a young man ambitious to discover the Secret of Right Living went to an old master to learn to "ride on the wind." Rather than teach him any technique, the master took him on as a servant. The young man lived at the master's side for ten years, and at the end of that time he no

101

longer cared for profit or loss or coming or going, nor cared whether he cared, nor even knew; then he could ride on the wind. Pilots who ride on the wind enter the story through the back door; first they ride, then they forget about profit and loss and about themselves.

The oldest form of aerial travel is ballooning, which was first practiced in the eighteenth century, though accurately theorized about in the sixteenth. The occupants of a free balloon control only their ascent and descent. So far as their course over the ground is concerned, they are blown about like clouds. Because they are one with the wind, they feel no wind.

But, to use a marine analogy, if a balloon is a drifting raft, a hang glider or sailplane is a surfboard. It remains aloft by virtue of its forward motion, and it is always descending. The art of designing sailplanes is the art of making them descend as slowly as possible; the art of flying them is that of seeking out air masses whose upward movement cancels out the sink of the sailplane. The gliding pilot is a detective of Holmesian proportions, a stalker who can sniff out lift—odorless, invisible lift—and track it. Soaring at its best draws upon the ultimate refinements of the pilot's intuition and the engineer's art. Champion soaring pilots fly ships that have a beauty, compounded of function and sensual grace, such as is ordinarily found only in the creations of nature.

Soaring is a pleasure accessible to everyone. Ballooning, on the other hand, is an expensive, esoteric sport practiced by very few, and its paraphernalia are like illustrations from an old book. The men who ride balloons and gliders are, however, addicted to the same narcotic—the remote, abstracted dreaminess of solitary flight.

6. Hang Gliding

HANG gliding germinated quietly in the chemical-filled skies of Los Angeles and the cliff regions of the California coast. Out of the restless culture that brought the world the dune buggy and the desert motorcycle racer came this curious, gentle anomaly. It could have started as a counter-reaction to the widespread assault on nature with machine-driven things on wheels. But more likely, it simply developed from a strange, cyclic contagion let loose upon the world by spores of the kind that infected Otto Lilienthal and the Wright Brothers with a yen to fly years ago. The fact that it provided another, less expensive avenue for thrills obviously didn't hurt the cause, but psychologists might find an underlying widespread hunger for a new form of physical prowess, of proof of mettle.

Whatever the cause and origin, the vigor with which hang gliding is flourishing and the rapidity with which it is spreading across the country suggest the arrival of a sport epoch of broad dimensions. And how often does anyone get in on the beginning of an epoch? From California to Cape Cod, people are launching themselves into the sky aboard light, portable gliding rigs of every conceivable size and shape from Rogallo "kites" to gossamer-skinned tailless biplanes.

From the first tentative flights off gentle seaside sand dunes, adventure-struck hang glider pilots have zoomed off everything from the edge of the Grand Canyon, in Arizona, to high mountains in other states. From the first fragments of flight that lasted lucky seconds between launch and crunchdown, the hang-gliding legions have progressed to flights lasting hours in thermal updrafts.

Along the edge of a cliff, a hang glider sets up his machine.

The joy of hang gliding is that anybody with the inclination, courage, and cooperative geography can do it. The cost of equipment ranges from a few dollars to the neighborhood of $500, depending on whether one builds it or buys it. Furthermore, the sport so far has managed to avoid the heavy web of restrictions that brings every other kind of airborne activity under the all-encompassing embrace of the Federal Aviation Administration.

To become a hang glider pilot, one need not take a federally prescribed physical exam by a designated physician, as must aspiring airplane or soaring pilots. One need not log forty hours or so under the tutelage of a licensed flight instructor or pass a written exam and flight test. One need not be at least of a certain age. One need merely summon up sufficient audacity to put faith in an aerodynamic vehicle that is suspended by capricious breezes, controlled by body English, and monitored by simple human instrumentation like ears, eyes, and cheeks.

The penalty for those pilots who don't measure up can be anything from skinned knees to broken legs or wrists. In the first few years of the sport's growth, a handful paid with their lives, though most of these did so flying behind some kind of aerial tow, which introduces an extra element of hazard to hang gliding. The half-spoofing caveat offered beginners is, don't fly any higher than you'd care to fall.

You don't really develop the knack until you launch yourself into clear air. The best place to do this seems to be at the seashore, from high, sandy bluffs favored with steady, gentle sea breezes. This way, the fledgling flier has altitude, wind, an open, obstacle-free takeoff and landing zone, and a reasonably yielding surface to land on.

Pity the poor student pilots who must learn on the hard turf at the side of a mountain. They run valiantly downhill, their Rogallo wings steadied from behind by their instructors; they lift off and plummet a toe's reach above the grass maybe 20, 40, or 60 feet, and then settle to earth hard, their legs pumping, often stumbling to a crunching halt with the kite nosing over ignominiously.

The badge of achievement among these pilots is a symmetrically spaced set of raw skin patches along ribs, knees, and elbows.

The time to graduate to the top of the mountain can be as short as a few weekends, depending on the talent of the learner and his or her ability to sense and control what the glider is doing. As one young flier put it, having consummated superb giant flights from the very top of the ski hill at Mount Cranmore in New Hampshire after only five weekends of practice, "I just keep the nose of the kite somewhere between the stall and a nosedive. I guess I have a kind of feel for it."

While most of the local hang-gliding corps are skimming down the slopes a few feet or a few yards above the hillside, this young gentleman comes lofting off the highest point of the mountain and reaches the bottom of the hill while still 100 feet or so in the sky, well above the roof of the three-storey ski lodge. He then executes a flawless 180-degree swooping turn, kills off the last treetop-high chunk of altitude, and flares to a neat two-point, standing landing on the grass in front of the crowd.

Engulfed by waves of admiration, curiosity, and amazement from the onlookers, he spends the next half hour folding up his glider and happily fielding questions, appraising the requests from young ladies for flight instruction.

What is the kit made of? Where did he buy it? Did he build it himself? How does he maneuver the craft? The questions buzz around every arrival who successfully skims onto the base plateau. As with hang gliding's nautical counterpart, surfing, the sport draws as many or more enthralled spectators as it does participants. The ski slopes in summer offer a nearly ideal gliding format, with lifts operating to haul fliers and their rigs up the mountainside. The only major problem posed by Eastern ski mountains, in particular, is that some have rather narrow, tree-lined corridors for hang gliders to negotiate, with strange turbulent eddies generated from surrounding forests.

Ski-slope operators try to solve the liability problem by having hang glider pilots sign releases. But they do encourage their coming, since hang gliding may draw life-sustaining crowds during the summer season.

At first (below) the glider descends as it picks up airspeed, but airspeed means lift, which causes the glider to rise (top, opposite) until settling again toward the ground.

By far the dominant type of hang glider throughout the country is the Rogallo, a triangular contraption whose main elements are two leading edge wing bars and a center keel bar with a dacron "sail" spread between them. A vertical kingpost and a cross tube hold the wings outstretched at the proper angle (just under 90 degrees at the nose), and the pilot fastens himself onboard by means of a seat sling or prone riding sling. He rides just behind and holds onto the base of a triangular trapeze bar, which controls the flight path of the Rogallo.

The standard Rogallo has no control surfaces like ailerons or rudder; the flier banks and alters pitch angle by manipulating the trapeze bar. To pitch the nose of the craft up for a climb or a landing flare, he pushes the trapeze bar out ahead of him; to drop the nose, he pulls back. To turn left, he thrusts the bar to the right, in effect swinging his own weight to the left, and so forth.

Francis M. Rogallo developed the Rogallo flex wing, as it is sometimes called, in the late 1940s, and NASA devoted considerable research toward making it into a space reentry vehicle that could be collapsed like an umbrella at high velocities, then unfurled as a kind of low-lift wing to allow a long glide down to a controlled landing.

Its main shortcoming is a modest lifting efficiency, or glide ratio, of not better than 4 to 1 at best, compared with 20 or 30 to 1 in sophisticated competition sailplanes and 9 to 1 among the best airplane-like hang gliders. Its chief advantages are simple construction and reasonably forgiving stall characteristics. Unlike a conventional airplane, the Rogallo does not tend to pitch nose down abruptly with the loss of lift caused by a stall (when the angle of attack is too high). Instead, it tends to mush down with the nose still raised, like its aerodynamic cousin, the controllable parachute.

Gusty winds present the Rogallo, and most of the other hang gliders for that matter, with their most serious challenge. Since the glider flies no more than 15 to 25 mph, a sharp gust of 5 to 10 mph can subject the craft to an instant stall situation. The modest body-weight control system of the Rogallo allows the pilot too slow a correction in some situations. The result can be calamitous at low elevations. Hence, experienced hang glider pilots avoid flying in turbulent conditions.

Ironically, the one other major area of piloting concern occurs when inexperienced hang gliders are coursing downhill with a good margin of altitude in fine, still air. They tend to dive out of control into the ground occasionally, for no apparent reason. The cause has been traced to the deceptive appearance of groundspeed at high altitude, where the pilot senses that he is moving more slowly. He dives downward to pick up airspeed and loses control.

For strength, most Rogallos now are constructed of aluminum tubing framework and stainless steel cables, covered with a dacron sail cut to prevent luffing. They fold into the dimensions of a dinghy sail for portability. The 40-pound overall weight permits the pilot to lug the entire apparatus uphill without much strain.

In one form or another hang gliding has sputtered along throughout the years, thanks to the research and testing of fliers like Otto Lilienthal in Germany and Octave Chanute in the United States at the end of the nineteenth century, and then the Wright Brothers and John Montgomery after the turn of the century. It was the Rogallo, however, which provided the technical spark that touched off the current blossoming of interest in the sport. The first stirrings occurred in the 1960s, as young men like Richard Miller and Dave Kilbourne stepped off the smooth bare California hills, slung under crude contraptions, and taught themselves to glide. Early Rogallos, built of wood or bamboo and sheet plastic, suspended pilots by their armpits from parallel bars.

In 1970 and 1971, the sport picked up new momentum with the involvement of innovative craftsmen like Dick Eipper, Taras Kiceniuk, and Volmer Jensen. Eipper specialized in Rogallos, while Kiceniuk developed a tailless biplane called Icarus II that produced an admirable glide ratio of 8 to 1. Jensen, an old-timer in hang gliding as well as other areas of aviation, developed a superb airplane-like hang glider in monoplane configuration, with a tail, and called it the VJ-23 Swingwing. Its as yet unsurpassed glide ratio is 9 to 1, and the craft has fairly conventional controls: ailerons, rudder, elevator.

With the sport well through its initial stage, the trend is toward evolving ever-more sophisticated designs that provide more lift and better controllability. Rogallos with higher aspect ratios (longer wings and shorter fore-and-aft span) are appearing as rigid-framed wings with rib-formed airfoils. Many of the pioneer designers have formed companies that sell plans, kits, and complete hang gliders.

Such is the booming enthusiasm for the new sport that dozens of companies have sprung up offering kites and kite components. The great hazard here for the novice is in not selecting designs that are safe, strong, and airworthy.

The Federal Aviation Administration so far has adopted a hands-off policy, offering no guidance and imposing no controls on the design of hang gliders as it does on conventional sailplanes and powered aircraft. The only involvement of the FAA in the hang-gliding movement is that it issued an advisory circular suggesting that fliers loft no more than 500 feet above the general terrain, stay out of control zones and airport traffic areas without permission, and steer at least 100 feet horizontally away from buildings and crowds. In typical fastidious legalese, it also requests that hang gliders remain clear of clouds.

At any rate, the only way for aspiring hang glider pilots to gauge the merit of the various designs and equipment is to glean the information from people already active in the sport, from hang-gliding clubs, and from the various publications on the subject. The best known of these books is called *Low and Slow*, published in Venice, California (at 59 Dudley Avenue), and edited by Joe Faust. It is packed with information on the latest equipment and trends in the hang-gliding world. The Soaring Society of America, which for years concerned itself with developments in the sophisticated, slightly rarefied air of the competition sailplane, has showed its true ecumenical colors by embracing the new "ultra-light" aircraft wholeheartedly. This organization, which publishes a handsome monthly magazine on soaring, offers an information kit to beginning hang gliders. Its address is Box 6601, Los Angeles, California 90069.

Naturally, with growth comes organization, and hang glider groups are appearing all around the country. Foremost among these is the Southern California Hang Glider Association, located at Box 246, Lomita, California,

HANG GLIDING

As hang gliding has increased in popularity, more and more areas have opened to it. Skiing areas, with their slopes, are especially attractive to hang gliders.

90717. On the east coast, the Boston Sky Club at Box 375, Marlboro, Massachusetts, has hoisted its colors as a rallying point among sky surfers.

In May of 1971, the first full-fledged hang-gliding meet was held. Jack Lambie, a young California high-school teacher whose class built a Chanute-type glider from ancient plans, was one of the moving forces of this first Otto Lilienthal Soaring Meet, held in Corona del Mar, south of Los Angeles.

Although only a couple of dozen gliders appeared, the event served to bring together the diverse hang-gliding trends then developing, and to offer food for thought about future projects. Since then, succeeding Lilienthal meets and others in California have drawn hundreds of pilots and thousands of spectators. In 1974, the British held their first hang-gliding meet. Quite appropriately, a large international meet was held that same year at Kitty Hawk, where, some years back, a couple of glider pilots, the Wrights, went on to more ambitious undertakings with smelly, clattering, gas-burning engines.

How intriguing it is that three-quarters of a century later, after a decade capped by rocket hops to the moon and supersonic transport leaps across the Atlantic in three hours, science is turning back upon itself in ultra-slow, ultra-light flight. Who can predict what alchemy will result from this strange blending of diverse elements: pure abstract science and the hearty, grunting, sweat-filled world of the sport hang glider? Certainly all the signs point toward a profitable union. The batttered biosphere can well afford to encourage any pursuit that assails neither the pure sky nor man's tranquil perception of it.

If the result is nothing more than a new excuse for international camaraderie and a common effort to tease the wind to gentle obedience, it might be worth it.

7. *Soaring*

Few flying things are more majestic than a sailplane which is flown well. The gracefulness of a sailplane's movement makes engineless flight seem more natural than flight under power. Surely for the pilot it is the easiest thing in the world. As this soaring pilot indicates, however, the matter is a bit complex:

"Smoke in the cockpit! You've scarcely felt the tremor of your plane's wings before the acrid smells of burning rubber, paint, and hot metal fill its tiny compartment. A glance at the instrument panel confirms what your senses discovered for themselves. You're delighted; the shiny spots of perspiration on the stick evaporate, your breathing deepens, and the muscles of your back and buttocks settle again in the seat's contours. Considering the circumstances, a power pilot might find such reactions curiously inverted. For him, smoke in the cockpit would signal danger: 'Land if you can—quick!' For you whose aircraft is a motorless sailplane, it means rescue: 'You won't be forced to land after all—here's lift!'

"You drop the wing to spiral and gunsight its leading edge on the flickering yellow flames of a trash dump, the source of the noxious fumes. Now you can see it, a faint pillar of blue-white smoke angles down to burning piles of refuse 700 feet below. The column had eluded you because, from above, its color blended with the light shades of surrounding hills. In addition, thanks to an unnoticed wind shift, it tilted and rose where you least expected it to. As a result, fruitless probing above the fire cost you precious altitude until you stumbled into the updraft during a desperate, wide sweep.

Lightness and sleekness are the essential ingredients of sailplane design.

"Sight, smell, and touch (through the seat of the pants) found what instruments had not, a rising core of heated air, a thermal. The thermal is narrow but fairly strong; to climb, you rely on variometers (ultra-sensitive rate-of-climb indicators) to help you center your spiral in the lift. Nevertheless, as you circle upward, you experience the gratification of having 'felt' the surrounding air through your own bodily sensors rather than with the panel's electronic and mechanical gadgetry. This is the essence of soaring.

"Don't misunderstand. No one's knocking power. It's fun transportation that carries a pilot through the air with great aplomb. But the man who—since boyhood, perhaps—has hankered to lift his feet from the earth's clay doesn't want to fly *through* so much as *in* the air. For him, following an engine around as it ravages the sky turns out to be a deception of sorts. The powered plane, which was to have been his means, may become an end—a jealous, demanding engine that seduces attention, effort, and loyalty, and alienates his longing for intimacy with the wind. He finds himself (if he thinks about it) insulated from nature's sky by vibration, noise, horsepower, electronic navigational aids, machinery.

"How odd that artisans who fashioned hull and sail for ancient vessels failed to invent the glider—a basically simple machine. The development of powered aircraft had to await the technologies of metal, engine, and electronics. Fabric and wood were nonetheless available in the time of the Pharaohs, and, except for a few bits of metal (replaceable with a little ingenuity), an ancient tinker could have built a 'primary glider' of the 1920s; if he had pulled an oar or skipped a rock on the Nile, he could also have understood the primary's simple aerodynamic logic.

"These crude craft were little more than a wing trussed to an open framework carrying a pilot. They coasted—glided—down hills on short flights of a few minutes, after which they had to be laboriously dragged to the top to repeat the process. The slope of descent, the glide angle, was rather steep, and they were unable to use rising currents to gain altitude. To do this—to soar instead of glide—the framework was enclosed, rigging was eliminated, and wing shapes were lengthened and refined until glider was transformed into sailplane.

"Decades separate the German-built sailplane that lofts you above the trash fire from those early primary gliders, but they are still sisters under the skin, and present-day usage makes no distinction between the terms 'sailplane' and 'glider.' To the soaring pilot, the most important difference is 'L/D.' L/D means lift-to-drag ratio, and is the aerodynamicist-designer's way of saying that at a 5,000-foot altitude, the average modern sailplane would fly almost 30 miles toward the horizon, compared to 7 or 8 miles for a primary.

During an air-towed takeoff, the sailplane remains earthborne only briefly and is usually off the ground well before the towplane.

"A sailplane can be a thing of beauty. The builder has conspired with the wind to loft lines that loosen the clutch of air drag and gravity and give the ship a nice, flat glide angle. The resulting curves and slender wings not only serve this functional purpose but have been known to evoke an admiration reserved for pure sculpted form.

"The L/D figures of the best current sailplanes are in the 40s. The state of the art in fiberglass technology and composite structures now permits artisans to handcraft wings the surface contours of which are true to the design airfoil within a thousandth of an inch or less. Instead of being shouldered aside by rivet heads, fabric seams, and so forth, the layer of air molecules next to the skin rolls along smoothly. The neighboring strata are hardly disturbed and bend aside, instead of breaking ranks to resist the wing's passage with turbulence.

"On metal skins, a 'filler' to smooth out blemishes can prove harder to apply than the skillful makeup of a beauty queen. One active pilot has complained in print of spending as much time filling and sanding the wings of his sailplane as flying.

"Dust that settles between wipe-off and takeoff can be an irritant. A contestant at the U.S. Soaring Championships sought to beat this problem by encasing his wings in long, stocking-like covers, which his crew whipped off just before the towplane began its roll. (His efforts were for naught, however: he later ran into a swarm of insects whose gossamer remains on the leading edge noticeably eroded his L/D.)

"Even smog can gum up the works. The crew of a power ship experimenting with boundary-layer control was mystified when separation occurred in a wing already operating in laminar mode. Subsequent investigation revealed that descent into concentrations of microscopic pollutants had disrupted the flow. Instruments recording the aircraft's performance alerted the crew to the change.

"Human ears can also spot clues. Standing blindfolded on a 200-foot

There is no end to the work of keeping a sailplane in good shape, but the work is part of the fun.

cliff overlooking the Pacific, two enthusiasts once amused themselves during a sailplane meet by competing to see which could identify—by sound only—the larger number of ships. It's possible to recognize a specific sailplane by the unique combination of whistles, hisses, and swishes it makes while passing overhead.

"'I don't have to watch my boys scrimmage to tell how well they're playing,' a famous football coach is supposed to have said. 'I can close my eyes and hear.' He measured the quality of his team in direct proportion to the volumes of sound generated by the violent contact of pad, muscle, and bone. In a way, the same can be said of a sailplane, except that here the relationship is inverse—the less the sound, the better the glider.

"Even the sleekest modern design makes a little noise. Not noise, really: the sound has a special timbre—like an orchestration without dissonance. The smooth strands of its texture are music to the attuned ear; the

A sailplane cockpit is small and highly efficient, with a large canopy to keep things warm under the sun.

The business end of a Waco UPF-7.

Three of sport flying's magnificent machines: a balloon, a classic restoration, and a sailplane, piloted by George B. Moffat.

J. K. West's gutsy old B-25.

Frank Tallman flying
a Grumman J2F-2 in *Murphy's War*.

ABOVE: One of the most exciting aerobatic teams is that of
Larry Kingry and Harry Shepard flying Waco Meteors.

OPPOSITE ABOVE: At Cleveland, gaudy unlimiteds lined up on the ramp.

OPPOSITE BELOW: Most of the work in ballooning is on the ground.

BELOW: The overwhelming Fairey Firefly.

Canada's showpiece formation team, the Snowbirds, in their Avro Tutors.

sounds produced by pitot tubes, fairings, ill-fitting canopy enclosures, hatch covers, wheel wells, and other assorted protuberances are discords.

"For some, happiness is a silent cockpit. In high-performance sail-planes, pilots frequently try to mute these noises (and thus lessen drag) by using plastic tape to seal gaps. However, by doing this they eliminate an important sensor that works at both conscious and subconscious levels. Now they must be willing continually to monitor their airspeed dials, or they may hear a new sound disturbing the quietude as did a South African pilot recently.

"He had been intent upon an approaching airport. His ultra-high-performance sailplane was not supposed to exceed 250 kilometers per hour, and for this reason he felt no uneasiness when a section of a small table with flight figures obscured that portion of his airspeed indicator above 280 kph.

"In a plane that is well sealed, one detects practically no change in the noise level as the airspeed changes. The pilot noticed that the hand of the airspeed indicator had disappeared. He moved the stick back gently, and suddenly at his right there was a small noise, like a rat gnawing timber. And then he saw his right wing fold back like a jackknife.

"Luckily, he was able to get clear of his ship and open his chute.

"Not all sailplanes are so quiet as the South African's. Climbing above the trash fire you listen to sound messages filtering into the cockpit. When a sudden rush like blowing across a milk bottle breaks the treble hiss flowing past the canopy, you know you are entering the core of the thermal. This is the region of greatest lift, and its boundary is well defined. The sailplane's structure creaks a little at the upward thrust. Within seconds, the variometers confirm the increase in climb. Since this core is narrow, and since it meanders in its invisible ascent, you must continually search and probe. It is impossible to set up a coordinated turn that describes a true circle without wandering from the lift; intuition dictates a skid here or a slip there as the easiest way to regain the elusive center. This calculated sloppiness superimposes new sounds on old, so that there are counterpoints of speed, flight attitude, and lift to untangle.

"At 2,000 feet, the flow of sound breaks up into gusty throbs; the thermal's steady lift has changed to bubbly turbulence. You recognize the

A classic American sailplane, the Schweizer 1-26.

message: top floor—elevator stops here! In the same way that cigarette smoke spreads across a ceiling after rising in the stillness of an empty room, the updraft is being stopped by a different sort of ceiling, a temperature inversion. Normally, as you climb, the outside air thermometer registers a drop of about 3.5 degrees Fahrenheit for each 1,000 feet of altitude. Now you have bumped into a warm layer that has erased the temperature difference between the ascending current and the surrounding atmosphere. It's like turning off a switch. You can climb no higher, but you are content because you had 'read' the air directly; altimeter, varios, and thermometer corroborate what you have physically perceived.

"That is not all you perceive. Above the land, your mind's eye sees a shadowy pageant of continuous change. Here is a realm of living weather; a kaleidoscopic panorama of variety, richness, and challenge; a three-dimensional arena where each hour can mean a new confrontation. It sharpens your sense for clues that may lead you to the exhilarating lift that means flight and freedom. Perhaps your eye is caught by an imperceptible gradation of blueness in the haze against the mountain. A closer look reveals a sight beyond the wildest imaginings of a surfer. Gliding toward the area, you squint into the deep blue above and see wraithlike vapor shadows. A gigantic tidal wave of air is pouring down the escarpment onto the valley floor! You know you will be witness to—no, a part of—a conflict in nature that the earthbound immediately below are not even aware is going on.

"If you stay sharp, you will ride millions of tons of dry, clear desert air forced aloft by opposing heavy, moist marine air from the ocean. Abruptly, you feel a series of small palpitations; again the hiss of air past the canopy breaks, but this time in a different rhythm from the thermal top-out of the trash fire. Maybe there is a smooth upward push, or a sharp, turbulent slap; but a pilot doesn't need a variometer to know he has contacted the 'shear line.' Man and machine are carried up thousands of feet in a tremendous surf of air.

"Immense as this battle of air masses seems to the soaring pilot, it is too small to be noted on U.S. Weather Bureau maps. These charts are concerned with vast continental 'systems,' while the shear line is a facet of micrometeorology. Like tides of the ocean, local diurnal air rivers ebb and flow between desert and sea. The contention of marine and desert air masses produces a sort of aerial riptide that represents soaring opportunity.

"Sometimes, city smog is borne along with the ocean haze, making the line quite visible and easy to find. At other times, the line of demarcation is vague. Does it run straight, or is it a coastline with bays and promontories? Is it moving along the ground or does it stand still? No instrument answers these questions; the pilot arrives at his answers tactually—by feeling his way in the invisible structure of the air.

"A straight, well-formed shear line is a joy to the cross-country flier. Instead of having to search for thermals, dust-devils, or other sources of lift, he soars along the edge without having to stop and circle for altitude. Under such conditions, high-performance sailplanes in the hands of skilled pilots have been known to outspeed light aircraft over considerable distances.

"In winter, large high-pressure systems pass north of the valley. The overflow spills onto the basin and pushes up the escarpment, providing slope winds for ridge soaring. Historically, this was the first mode of soaring flight, and for many pilots it remains the most exciting. Under marginal conditions, the pilot finds himself a wingspan away from precipice, ravine, or rock. At one moment he may skim the treetops, while at the next he may launch himself over the void of a yawning chasm.

"This comes about as close to the feeling of pure flight as it's possible to get.

"The lore of gliding contains many fascinating tales growing out of this type of soaring: squadrons of buzzards join a sailplane in echelon formation; aggressive hawks hurl themselves in kamikaze attacks against the canopies of intruders. A practical joker approaches a military radar station on a remote peak; he stays below the ridge, chandelles into the teeth of the wind, and hovers motionless above the dome. 'Watch the door down there,' he tells his passenger. Within seconds, the radar crew bursts forth, their faces upturned to discover what manner of UFO has appeared so suddenly on their screen.

"A few miles farther along the ridge, he again swings into the wind and astounds U.S. Forestry personnel by backing his sailplane up the mountain side.

"When conditions are right, an air mountain the size of Everest can appear above the valley. As yet, its summit remains unconquered, though ascents of more than 4 miles up its flank have been made. Wave-soaring, as this kind of flying is called, is a variant of orographic lift (flow displaced by topography), and for some pilots the most exciting of all types of soaring. Oddly, this is accomplished by flying in what would normally be the down-flow side of a ridge or mountain. What happens is roughly analogous to wavy undulations of water caused by a large boulder just below the surface of a brook. The surface upstream is little disturbed, but downstream it breaks into a series of crests and troughs that gradually diminish and dampen out. Because of the compressibility of the air, the amplitude (height) of these displacements is proportionately much greater. Thus, when a strong flow from the Pacific pours down the escarpment, it may bounce to a Himalaya-sized rampart.

Puffy clouds result from vertical movement of the air—and to a soaring pilot that means beautiful lift.

"FAA regulations have made these heights off limits in the valley, but behind the Sierra, the government has left a few holes in the ceiling. It is through these that the ultimate confrontation will one day take place.

"In the predawn darkness, a yet-to-be-built pressurized sailplane will be towed to the base of a wave generated by a storm-front passage. After release, it will begin a climb that at times could exceed 2,000 feet per minute.

At some moment during the ascent, it will pass the present 46,000-foot record and continue upward—just how far remains to be seen. (A U-2 has contacted waves at 70,000 feet.) In bitter cold, it will turn away from the darkness of the west wind and toward the first light of dawn.

"From such altitudes, even if the wind were suddenly to cease, the world distance record of 1,000 miles would probably fall to a nearly straight glide. A study identified thirty-six wave sites on the two main controlled airways to the Rockies from the Los Angeles area. It is reasonable to suppose that the frequency and distribution in the uncontrolled airspace lying between is the same.

"With a strong following wind, the flight would ricochet eastward from wave to wave, whose distances apart are seldom as much as 100 miles. The secondary undulations trailing these primaries would provide additional stepping stones across the Western United States. Airline captains who are also soaring pilots have found upward components in the jet stream enabling them to maintain altitude at reduced power with 707s.

"The combination of wave, jet stream, and pressurized sailplane has given rise to more daydreaming than anyone is willing to admit. But someday a ship out of the West will appear high in the last wave above the Rockies' eastern slopes. Ahead, the open plains will beckon as far as the eye can see, and it will still be morning."

The elegant Schweizer 2-32.

8. *Competitive Soaring*

For most soaring pilots, the sheer fun of the sport lies in being up there, in the rush of the wind, treading the air alone and unreachable, concentrating on staying there, but strangely relaxed, happy. A minority of them, however, find joy in pressure, in self-created tribulation, in head-to-head combat, be it with pilots one can see or with pilots who are visible only as numbers in record books, numbers one seeks to replace with those of one's own. These are the competitors, the fine-honed pilots for whom being in the sky means being in an arena where they must fly better than anyone else in order to be happy.

There are essentially two kinds of soaring competition. One is the solitary sport of trying to fly farther or higher or longer than one has done oneself before—that's at the beginning—or than others have done. Included in such sport is the winning of various badges for particular achievements and endurance efforts that may demand the same physical fortitude as that of a marathon runner. The other major area is contest soaring, where one's opponents share the same skies and conditions and where psychology plays as important a part in winning as does piloting prowess.

It is not unusual for pilots to engage in both kinds of competition. Richard Johnson, of Dallas, Texas, is an example. An easygoing, amiable man,

125

he has been eight times U.S. national champion and has made several significant distance flights. Part of the motivation lies in the pleasure of winning or of flying under pressures beyond the ordinary. And part of it lies in the fact that the fraternity of competitive pilots is relatively small. The élite all know each other and take a brotherly satisfaction in beating each other when they can.

The first American national champion was not crowned until 1930. The first world championship meet was held in 1937. However, soaring competition had been going on long before that. The original competition was, of course, against gravity. To fly longer than a few seconds or a dozen feet was goal enough. But during the 1920s, as gliders became more sophisticated and pilots more understanding of such things as the causes of lift, their aims could be broadened and lengthened.

Not surprisingly, the earliest competition involved distance and duration. The sailplanes would set off, grasp as much altitude as they could get, and go as far or stay up as long as they could. They did this largely by ridge soaring at first, but as they learned to work thermals efficiently and then discovered the wave effect, they began to expand their distances and times considerably.

In effect, every soaring pilot begins as a competitor. The Fédération Aéronautique Internationale, a worldwide organization that has regulated sport and record flying since 1905, has set standards of achievement to which every pilot may aspire; the highest of these involve silver, gold, and diamonds. To win a silver badge, for instance, a pilot must fly at least 50 kilometers (31.1 statute miles) on a straight-out course; he must remain aloft at least five hours; he must gain a height of at least 1,000 meters (3,281 feet) over the altitude at which he is released from his tow. These three requirements do not, of course, cover the same flight, but more than one requirement may be fulfilled on any given flight. To win a gold badge, a pilot must fly a distance of at least 300

OPPOSITE. Wearing a tennis hat for protection against the sun, a soaring competitor waits for the canopy of his ship and the towrope to be installed.

kilometers (186.4 sm), remain aloft at least five hours, and gain at least 3,000 meters of altitude (9,842 feet). Once one has earned his silver or gold badge, he may attach diamonds to it. One diamond represents a flight of at least 500 kilometers (310.7 sm); another signifies a journey of at least 300 kilometers over a triangular or out-and-return course; the third means that one has gained at least 5,000 meters (16,404 feet) of altitude.

Literally thousands of pilots have sought such badges over the years, and the roster of the many hundreds who have earned them reads like a *Who's Who* of soaring.

During the postwar years, when wave flight, sailplane design, and knowledge of aerodynamics all improved rapidly, record soaring flights quickly became at first monumental and then matter-of-fact tests of human ability to stay awake, unfrozen, or interested. The current world distance record is held by Hans-Werner Grosse, of West Germany: on April 25, 1972, he flew his AS-W12 sailplane 907.7 miles. In 1961, American Paul F. Bikle, in a Schweizer 1-23E, climbed 42,303 feet for a world altitude gain record that remains intact today. On the same flight he set a still-standing absolute altitude mark of 46,267 feet. It is conceivable that in the near future, pilots taking advantage of wave conditions will soar even higher and farther—a coast-to-coast flight across the United States is considered ever more feasible as the years progress.

To go for various badges, local, national, or world records, a pilot need only follow a well-laid-down procedure, assemble a crew to retrieve him if that becomes necessary, and make his attempt. Except for the representative of the FAI—in the United States, these are members of the National Aeronautic Association—his crew, and well-wishers, the record-seeking pilot makes his attempt in relative obscurity. There are no crowds to cheer him along as he approaches the end of his endurance with the record just within reach if he can hold on. And seldom does recognition come from anywhere outside the aviation press. In the cockpit, as his mind writhes under the weight of fatigue, his bladder aches for want of relief, his skin grows numb in the biting cold, and he falls back upon sheer desire and pride to keep him going, the pilot may not enjoy what he is doing at all while he holds on against these sensations and the fear that he may have bitten off more than he can chew. Yet if he makes it, if he flies that extra distance, those extra hours, that extra height, if *his* name and achievement are printed in the books, there is reward enough, though many record setters have later confessed to a sense of letdown once the effort was past. Not an unusual feeling, actually. Other athletes, as well as artists, politicians, and various people who must perform under pressure, attest to the same sense of deflation. But like these others who put themselves on the line, the pilots keep coming back to do more.

At the heart of soaring competition is the contest. It is more personal, more intense, probably more fatiguing, and unquestionably more fun than the much more solitary endeavor of record flying. Speed records are often set at contests, but the objective all eyes rest upon is that of beating the others, or at least of beating some others.

The earliest contests, in Europe and the United States, were simple tests of how far the pilots could fly. They would check the wind, launch, and fly as far as the wind and lift could carry them. Such contests prevailed through the 1950s and led to strange anomalies. The pilots would expect to land "off-field," that is, away from the departure airport. On they would fly, while their ground crews tried to stay in reasonably close proximity to their track, pulling trailers into which to stuff the gliders. Once a pilot ran out of altitude, he would land, would have a card signed by a local citizen, usually the farmer in whose field he had set down, and wait for his crew which, upon arriving, would dismantle the aircraft, put it into the trailer, and head back to the contest airport. The better pilots were penalized by this, for the longer they flew, the longer and more fatiguing was the drive back. It was a running joke in soaring competition that the better the pilot, the worse he ate while the contest was on.

In time, Paul Bikle, who has been an important figure in the development of competition soaring, worked out an arrangement called the "Cat's Cradle," which tested a pilot's ability to stay up and fly far without imposing enormously long retrievals. Various aiming points would be designated in the general area surrounding the contest airport, to which pilots could fly. Under fairly complex rules as to which turnpoints one could fly to and when, pilots had to do more than merely determine which way to go with the wind. Course strategies became more important. Yet the object remained the same: to cover as much distance as possible. To do this, one had to judge the weather, local lift conditions, timing, and his experiences as he flew to or near various turnpoints.

In the 1960s, speed became a more popular criterion of skill than endurance, and it has remained so. On a given day of a contest, be it local, regional, national, or world, a "task" will be set by the contest committee. The assignment will be made on the basis of the forecast weather. The task could be a distance one, such as a Cat's Cradle, but it is more usually a closed-distance course, that is, a flight to a point and then a return or, more likely, a triangular course. All the sailplanes fly the same course, so time becomes of the essence. The distances flown may vary from 100 kilometers to several hundred. Usually, the shorter the distance, the more intense the flying, since even slight mistakes loom larger when there is less time and distance over which to rectify them. Once the task is set and the pilots are told what it will be, the drama is set.

The pilots select their launch times according to what they expect the lift conditions to be during the day. Their crews assemble, wash and rub down the sailplanes, and line them up in the order of takeoff. To the side, towplanes

Before the race, the powerless ships are wheeled into position for departure.

await the signal to start their work. Into the cockpits go charts, oxygen bottles, snacks and drinks, hand-operated computers, pencils, and personal aids. After the pilot has climbed into the ship, his turnpoint cameras are tested and authenticated. The cameras take photos of the turnpoints to verify that the pilot has actually flown over them. This is a sophisticated method for preventing what little cheating may be attempted. Soaring is very much an amateur sport and offers virtually nothing in material rewards, even to champions. Cheating is sometimes tried, but its practitioners are quickly unmasked and undone with almost amused contempt by the other pilots and the officials.

After the competing sailplanes lift off and are released from the towplanes, they head for an imaginary window in the sky, which serves as the starting gate. A pilot's time through the gate is noted and he is on his way. If he is good enough to fly the course and get back to the home field, he will be timed as he crosses the finish line. If he is forced to land away from the field, he may return and start again for a "relight," should there be sufficient time. The fastest time for completing the course yields 1,000 points. Slower times get less, and "off landings" still less.

The techniques and stratagems of competition are many, as the pilots seek the best thermals, try for the best speed between thermals, work to keep

Just before takeoff the pilot makes an identifying photo with his turnpoint camera. It is a tense moment.

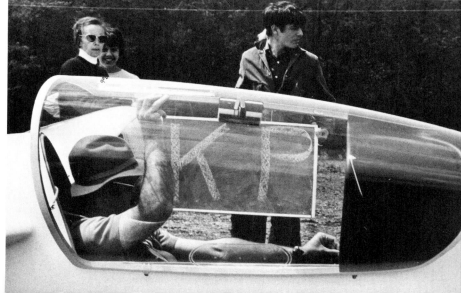

their competitors from taking advantage of good thermals, and also keep an eye open to help their teammates. Good thermals draw sailplanes to them like magnets once they are found, and "gaggles" of sailplanes form within them, circling above and below each other, striving for lift.

In the United States, yet another class has seen keen competition, in fact, the closest competition in soaring, because the pilots all fly the same model, the Schweizer 1-26. These sailplanes sell for about $6,000 new, well below the prices of standard and open-class planes, which can cost $10,000 and more.

Standard-class ships range from $8,000 to a little more than $10,000. Among the most prominent are the Schempp-Hirth Standard Cirrus and the Glasflugel Standard Libelle. The Torva Sprite and the Schleicher AS-W15 have also been in great demand. Their maximum speeds range around 135 to 137 mph. Hoping to capture the hitherto European-dominated standard-class market, the Schweizer Aircraft Corporation—the most prominent designer and manufacturer of sailplanes in this country for many years—has introduced the 1-35, a high-performance metal ship.

Among the open-class sailplanes, the Schempp-Hirth Nimbus II is the current leader. Its wingspan is nearly 67 feet and it can attain a maximum speed of 155 mph. Its closest competitors are the Schleicher AS-W17 and the Slingsby Kestrel 19.

One competition class is called "standard," and is composed of sailplanes whose wingspan can be no more than 15 meters (approximately 49 feet). The other class is called "open," and has no limitations upon its ships except prohibition of engines. Some of these ultra-high-performance ships have wingspans well over 60 feet. Most of the ships both in standard- and open-class competition are of fiberglass construction and carry water ballast in their wings. The weight of the water provides added speed in strong weather conditions. If a pilot feels he needs lift more than speed, he can "dump" the ballast.

The superships of the open class have become increasingly sophisticated, with the standards following close behind. Ultra-sensitive variometers, extremely accurate direction instruments, flaps, dive brakes, spoilers, and exquisite lines are the norm. One German plane, the SB-10, has a wingspan of more than 100 feet.

For all that, what *makes* soaring competition is the combination of weather, ship, and pilot along with psychological factors involving coolness, determination, and courage. The combination of these factors causes each meet to take on a personality of its own—sometimes an exaggerated one. As examples, one could take the two most recent world championship contests, one at Vršac, Yugoslavia, in 1972 and the other at Waikerie, Australia, in 1974. For sheer sporting drama, they would be hard to beat.

The contest at Marfa, Texas, in 1970, was ascetic by contrast. There were no spectators, no social centers. Sailplanes ranged silently over the empty task area of southwest Texas, competing for honors far from the few ground viewers and remote from each other. The clouds and the ancient volcanic hills of the Marfa plateau gave no hint of the sophisticated equipment, techniques, and certainly the pressures inherent in the top soaring competition. Vršac, Yugoslavia, 1972, was quite different. It was a competition deeply involved with people—with the inexperience of the organizers and their failures in communication, with the local populace stripping a cockpit of its equipment the minute a pilot walked away after a field landing. It was musicians who played at max volume, but superbly, in the evening and could not be persuaded to stop; policemen who were often officious or stupid; and the people who were injured and killed.

There have been championships before that have been run inefficiently, yet glider pilots are forgiving people. If the weather is fine and the flying good, most of the organizational frustrations somehow seem insignificant. But the weather at Vršac was the greatest—and most unexpected—disaster of all.

Thunderstorms persisted in the hazy, polluted air that circulates around Central Europe in summer. They were rarely isolated or simple: the storm cells coalesced most afternoons until much of the task area was blotted out by vast, amorphous cumulonimbus. With tops of 30,000 feet, bases at 2,500, solid rain to the ground, and nowhere to go, soaring required a will to survive even more than a will to win. And before the end, the storms had resulted in one death and a mid-air collision from which both pilots parachuted.

The first contest day was sunny. The task was a 326-kilometer triangle for the eighty-nine gliders making up the two classes, and the U.S. team started well. In the standard class, George Moffat, open-class world champion in 1970, came first in a Standard Cirrus, averaging 88 kph, with compatriot Ben Greene second in another Standard Cirrus. In third place was Helmut Reichmann of Germany, the defending standard-class champion, in an L.S.1. A. J. Smith made second place in the open class, just 8 kph slower than the day winner, Goran Ax of Sweden. Both flew Nimbuses.

A front to the northwest on the second day caused the organizers to plan a long race to the south, 456 kilometers to Bitolj—just short of Greece. Concern for safety obviously had not been paramount, since the last 80 kilometers of this race were over desolate mountains up to 8,000 feet high, where thunderstorms had been forecast. Some thirty pilots landed in or around Skopje—which would have been a sensible and safer goal flight of 352 kilometers—but others groped around the mountains trying to find a way through. Hauernstein, a Swiss entrant, mixed with cloud and mountains too much, and landed far into Bulgaria.

This time it was the U.S. open-class pilots who topped the field. Dick Johnson got nearest to the goal with 392 kilometers, closely followed by A. J. Smith. The top scorers in the standard class, Moffat and Greene, fell back to twentieth and twenty-sixth places respectively. Although a setback, it was not yet a calamity. Reichmann dropped to twelfth place, and Kepka of Poland, who eventually placed third in the final results, was right down at twenty-eighth.

The real contest was for the crews. At two hours' notice, they set out with their 30-foot trailers for the wild southern mountains, a journey of perhaps 1,600 kilometers. This was no interstate freeway drive. The people of Macedonia live on farm tracts, speak a different language, and have a different alphabet. They could not understand the "request assistance" cards that had been provided by the organizers. The police could not comprehend the situation; five pilots landing in one field were not allowed to speak to each other. Dick Johnson, trying to snatch a few hours' sleep in a local hotel, was awakened by police turning on all the lights in his room and inspecting him at close range for similarity with his passport photo. Nels Johnson, aged seventeen, crewing for his father, had only two packets of crackers and some wild berries to sustain him on the day it took to drive back.

No one was worried when the weather turned sour on the two days following Bitolj; there was too much to do getting equipment in shape again. But it then stayed gray and showery—only one unsuccessful attempt was made to get in a task—for the rest of the first week. With just two contest days achieved, the outlook was gloomy in the nearly saturated air and waterlogged ground. However, on July 16 the sky looked better and a 349-kilometer triangle was set for both classes. It was an odd day, one that caused the downfall of several top pilots. Cloudbase at Vršac was 9,000 feet and the day was hot and hazy. Without difficulty, pilots reached the cloudbase, dived down to cross the start line at 3,000 feet, and whistled back up to 8,000 feet or so before setting off. It seemed like proper high-speed soaring conditions at last.

But for many pilots, the first climb was all they got. West of Vršac, there were almost no thermals, and the cloudbase dropped abruptly to a mere 5,000 feet—when it could be seen at all. Moffat, Greene, Reichmann, and other fine pilots such as Rudensky of the U.S.S.R. and Nietlispach of Switzerland simply flew on in the dead-still air until the ground came up, landing before even reaching the first turnpoint. But there were some pilots who managed to be more wary, more patient, luckier, or even more skillful. They waited or somehow avoided the dead area, struggling along toward a cumulonimbus before the second turnpoint. It was a strange cloud, this one large, almost stationary, and with a slow, pulsing rhythm of growth, dispersion, and regrowth. Some pilots used it, went on to the turnpoint, and glided out along the last leg. A. J. Smith figured that mountain wave was modifying the convection, but the cloud was inactive when he arrived and he had to land. Only one pilot got home: Tabart, an Australian flying a Kestrel 17 in the open class, went back to the big cloud, having photographed the turnpoint, and found it sufficiently active to give him 11,000 feet. From this height, he set off on the 120-kilometer leg to Vršac, arriving at the finish line with 100 feet, and having found no help on the way. At the end of this day, Ragot of France was leading in the standard class, and Ax in the open, in total points for the meet.

Until now, the cumulonimbus had been isolated. On July 17, they grew larger, reaching 30,000 feet, and the space between them diminished. On the ground, humidity was high in the sultry air. Two triangles were set: 308 kilometers for the open class, and inside it, 213 kilometers for the standard. For the open pilots, it was especially difficult, because their second turnpoint farther south was blotted out by a massive storm. To return to Vršac it had to be used, but normally no pilot would have gone inside. Some took a bite and hurried out, wings and canopy iced, and landed short of the goal. Only Nick Goodhart of Britain, in a Kestrel 19, open class, made it back. He had climbed to 28,000 feet with a timed 10 minutes at 2,000 fpm. Nineteen pilots returned to Vršac from the shorter standard-class task, among them Ben Greene, who was only 8 kph slower than Nietlispach, the day winner. But it was this day that finally saw an end to the hopes of the two 1970 champions; both Moffat and Reichmann landed short, Reichmann only 34 kilometers out. One storm was extremely severe. Inside it, Voss of East Germany had his Cobra punctured all over with pigeon-egg-sized hail; not so lucky was Varkozi, a Hungarian, who had been flying with his compatriot Petroczy in the storm. He died when his Cobra crashed in a region where roofs had come off the houses and trees were blown down. In such conditions, apart from the solid wall of water blotting out everything, a normal landing would have been impossible. Some think he sustained a direct lightning strike at about 9,000 feet. In the face of such disaster, little notice was taken when, at the finish line, official observers were found uninjured after their radio antenna on the tower was struck by lightning, or of the plight of Denmark's Taarnhoj, who had his turnpoint evidence cameras stolen. Without them, he got no points.

During the next two days, the rumbling and lowering sky brought so much rain that trailers bogged on anything but main roads. The tiedown area on the field was underwater, and crews filling the sailplane water ballast tanks had to wade. The 5 tons of water used daily for this purpose only added to the flooded countryside.

With three days left, flying was again possible on July 20, but the weather did not relent. A 309-kilometer triangle was set to the northwest for the open class and 198 kilometers to the southwest for the standard. By mid-afternoon, the sky at Vršac was winter dark, and rain fell steadily from a half-dead cumulonimbus 48 kilometers across. Only four pilots got through it in the open class, headed by Viitanen of Finland in an AS-W17. Now, it was the standard class's turn to be unlucky. Only two pilots made it home: Reichmann and Ben Greene, both of whom badly needed a good day. But 20 percent of the competitors had not achieved the minimum distance of 100 kilometers, so the task could not count.

On the penultimate day, July 21, the meteorologists predicted more organized convection and each class was given an out-and-return race: 371 kilometers to the west for the open class, and 250 kilometers to the south for the standard. At last, flying operations seemed as though they might be straightforward. The jury had a long session to investigate protests about the acceptability of turnpoint photographs. The problem of whether or not a photograph complied with the evidence rules had been a source of complaint ever since the first day, when twenty-two pilots initially had their photographs discounted. Most of the trouble stemmed from the refusal of the organizers to use the approved system developed at Marfa, after having said in their local rules that they would. They allowed no adequate practice of evaluation in the use of their alternative system during the practice week, nor did they make master turnpoint photographs or diagrams freely available to pilots.

For the third time, only one pilot in the open class made it back—Viitanen, of Finland, in his AS-W17, landed at last light. It put him in overall first position 240 points ahead of Sweden's Ax—the eventual winner by a tiny margin of 37 points—with one day to go. Twenty standard-class pilots got back, including Moffat (third), Reichmann (sixth), with Ben Greene (ninth) trying to make up for his canceled success of the previous day, but placing too low to help his final standing.

So the last day came. The met men again predicted more organized cumulus—big but not runaway—and the organizers set the same 238-kilometer triangle for both classes. Both were wrong. A thunderstorm brewed over the airfield even as launching started at 1100, and the task was contrary to the ruling of the FAI code, which states that wherever possible, different tasks shall be set for each class. Visibility was poor and storms were growing fast. Within two hours, a collision in cloud was reported. Pattersson of Sweden, open class, bailed out safely. He had seen his Nimbus and the L.S.1 of Innes of Great Britain crash, and he had also seen another parachute. Innes broke one leg badly on landing, and to reach an ambulance, he first had to be carried, then moved by boat through floods. For a long time, reports of a third parachute persisted, and it was not until nearly midnight that this possibility could be discounted. Almost lost in the confusion was a report that the Nimbus of A. J. Smith—the most immaculate and polished sailplane at Vršac—had been reduced to wreckage when it hit a tree during landing, and that the pilot had been taken away by ambulance. Fortunately, Smith was only bruised, having misjudged his approach after being washed out of the storm with all instruments flooded. The unkindest cut was that his cameras were stolen, so he could receive no points. The same fate befell Bradney, the Australian, whose cockpit was completely stripped, including the parachute.

It is just as well that soaring is not a spectator sport, because world soaring championships traditionally do best in remote places—a good scrubland desert seems about the optimum. Dry air gives an 8,000- to 10,000-foot cumulus base without too much cloud, the unpopulated land is free of urban restrictions, and most dirt roads are good enough to retrieve trailers. The 1974 World Championships were based in Waikerie, a small town on the fringe of the central Australian desert; few people had heard of it until the world's top sailplane pilots homed in on it early in January that year.

The world came to Waikerie, which a year earlier had been a desert with blowing, gritty sand, to find it green and under water. The locals said, as they always do, that the weather was unusual. Normally, 9 inches of rain a year was their lot, but this year they had already been blessed with 27—and it was still raining.

Then, on January 15, patches of blue glimmered through the low overcast, and a task was set. The two classes, open and standard, were given the speed task over a triangular course of 269.2 kilometers (161.5 sm). Not a single pilot got back to the airfield, and the day ended with sixty-seven superbly polished sailplanes scattered about in muddy sheep paddocks and sodden scrub.

A feeling that the world championships were going to be a disaster could not be entirely suppressed even by the normally optimistic pilots. After two previous world events with atypical weather, it was beginning to seem that the best way to get your country irrigated was to invite the world to soar on your patch. Fortunately, the weather improved, allowing so much flying that after seven consecutive task days, pilots were glad to have a stable air day so they could catch up on some sleep. After this, a further four days of flying made these championships the greatest ever for the number of contest days flown—eleven, as compared to the previous nine-day record set at Marfa, Texas, in 1970.

Once the Australian sun dominated the scene, the flying was superb. The tasks were over either triangular or quadrilateral courses, the extra turnpoint of the latter serving to keep pilots clear of inhospitable scrub country. Course distances were 300 to 500 kilometers.

On January 20, however, a task of 707 kilometers (424 sm) was given for the twenty-eight pilots of the open class. This was the largest triangle ever assigned in world championships. The cloud base was expected to be at 6,500 to 7,000 feet—not particularly high—with the winds light from the northwest. The course first took the pilots west to Clare, then 350 kilometers east across desert and scrub to Nagiloc, on the Murray River, and then back to Waikerie paralleling the river, which was often hidden in its gum-tree-filled valley. This was a historic task, and excitement grew at Waikerie as radio rumors indicated that some pilots might make it home. Staring into the distance brought spots before the eyes; the spots finally resolved themselves into two sailplanes streaking for the airfield together after seven hours airborne. George Moffat of the United States, in his heavily ballasted Nimbus II, had overtaken François Ragot of France, in his more lightly loaded AS-W17. The two crossed the finish line within seconds of each other. Altogether, ten pilots flew the entire 707 kilometers. Two were from Germany: Klaus Holighaus, designer and pilot of his Nimbus II, and Hans-Werner Grosse, world distance record holder in an AS-W17. There were also two from France—Jean Pierre Cartry and Ragot—and one pilot each from Sweden (Goran Ax), Belgium (Bert Zegels), Austria (Andreus Haemmerle), Britain (John Delafield), and Australia (Anthony Tabart). Six of the successful sailplanes were Nimbus II's, each carrying 300 pounds of water ballast.

Before the start of the day, Moffat had already achieved his favorite position—first. Although Moffat was only second in elapsed time at 103.3 kph against Ragot's 104.5, his lead was beginning to show signs of being unchallengeable. Moffat and Ragot fly very differently, the latter with a flamboyance backed up by an excellent technical understanding and a quick brain. Moffat flies consistently, like a fine machine. He wins because he makes the fewest wrong, or even slightly incorrect, decisions. Soaring, especially in top competition, continuously demands decisions from the pilot, but not many pilots are able to concentrate right on the top line for seven hours. Moffat can.

History was made again on January 24, when the two classes were given the same task: a 513-kilometer (308-sm) triangle. The course was southeast to Karoonda, northeast to the irrigated vineyard town of Mildura, and then a return to Waikerie. No less than sixty-four out of the sixty-six pilots flying that day got back; fifteen of them beat world record speeds, some by a handsome margin. Ax was fastest in the open class with 140.2 kph (84.12 mph); Moffat's speed was 136.8 kph, and Dick Johnson's 133.4. Even the slowest open pilot, Istvan Wlassics of Sweden, exceeded 100 kph. Moffat stayed in overall first place. Unfortunately, this triangle was not an "official FAI" course, and so new records could not be claimed. One turnpoint of an "official" course would have had to be nearer the coast, and the organizers feared that an encroachment of sea air might submerge the point, cutting off thermals. In any event, the sea did come in as a massive cumulus convergence zone lying just to the south of the return track, providing an impressive backdrop to the sailplanes streaming over the finish line. When most of them were back, however, the convergence zone moved overhead, bringing gusting winds of 25 knots, causing pilots and crews to check their tiedowns. Five minutes later, they were running in the opposite direction to lock their cars after the police announced that two convicts had escaped and were looking for wheels!

In the standard class, the pilots had not been given a giant-size task on January 20, merely a 308-kilometer (185-sm) triangle. This was an "FAI" course, meaning that pilots could claim national records if they went fast enough—and seven of them did.

The intention was that the standards would have a very big task on the following day, but the weather did not quite live up to expectations, and so they missed out. On January 24, thirty-six of the thirty-eight standard pilots got back, but only the winner's speed reached world record level. On this day, Tom Beltz of the United States came in third. At twenty-two, he was the youngest competitor in his first world championships—although he was something of a veteran, having been flying since he was fourteen. Crewed by his mother and father, both of whom are sailplane pilots, Tom has a relaxed approach to the tensions of competition that should ensure him a good future.

The fourth U.S. pilot, Ben Greene, was not so happy. Basically a big-span, open-class pilot, he found the "sports car" competition in the smaller, lighter standard-class ships not really his scene. Although any good pilot can fly open- or standard-class aircraft, they tend to fly in that class with which they feel more in tune. Pilots transferring from standard to open class usually have no problem, but going the other way does not seem to work as well. The classic case was in 1958, when Philip Wills of Britain had to fly standard for the first time and made nothing of the contest. In 1972, Moffat changed from open, in which he was reigning world champion, to standard and did not do so well. This year, back in open, he again became world champion. Sometimes a pilot changes classes out of choice, but more often it is because those higher on the seeding list of their country can choose first, and pilot number four has to take what is left. Ben Greene did not, in fact, do too badly, placing ninth. One of the few world distance record holders, he is a fine pilot on any count.

Competition in the standard class is usually closer than in the open. Standard is numerically larger; its pilots are on the average, at thirty-three, five years younger than those in open. But the most significant factor is probably the performance similarities of the aircraft. On the first day of the championships, the French pilots Penaud and Michel Mercier were on top, with Ingo Renner of Australia fifteenth and Helmut Reichmann of West Germany far down the list. By halfway through, Mercier was still first, with Walter Gordon of New Zealand second, and Bernard Fitchett of Britain third. Closing the gap, Renner had climbed into sixth place and Reichmann to fourth. With only one day to go, Renner reached first, with Reichmann second, and Fitchett glued into the third place he had held for over a week. Mercier was now fifth, but only 250 points out of 8,500 separated all of them. It was still anybody's championship, but then Reichmann just worked those very few vital added kph out of the last day to win. Renner was second, and Franciszek Kepka, of Poland, barely overtook Fitchett for third place.

It is rare for a pilot to become world champion more than once, but Waikerie saw it happen twice, both Moffat and Reichmann having won at Marfa in 1970. The two championships were not dissimilar. Southwest Texas is remote and wild like south-central Australia; at both places the cloudbases and speeds were high, and the tasks big and demanding.

The champions at Waikerie, Australia: George B. Moffat, Jr. (left), unlimited-class world titlist, and Helmut Reichmann, standard-class victor.

The championships at Waikerie were happy. The few permanent buildings on the airfield were supplemented by good-quality portable houses. Laid out close to the center were small mobile homes for key personnel and a "village square" of trailers for the use of the teams from each country. This congenial and practical arrangement was made even better by the close location of the big scoreboard and the outside bar, with its colorful umbrellas, giving a grandstand view of the finish line. It was a happy competition because it was also a safe one. Apart from one rear fuselage, only undercarriages and their doors suffered; the workshops at night were mostly empty.

As with most championships, the organization at Waikerie was largely voluntary, manned by members of the Gliding Federation of Australia, who had worked on the project for three years in their spare time. Transport to Australia and back had been provided on concession fares by Qantas. Some fifty cars were loaned to the event, and local wine cellars provided the parties. But the weather, having allowed such superb soaring, played prima donna at the end. After the clear evening of the last contest day, the prizegiving morning saw the heavens open. Rain fell heavily all day, with a strong wind. The ceremony, held in the hangar, was inaudible for the water drumming on the roof. Within hours, the airfield was flooded.

The 1974 championships were technically interesting. The standard class flew under new rules that permitted simple flaps. Only two ships had been specially so designed, the German LS-2 and the Finnish Pik-20. Both had their flaps hinged from the wing lower surface, drooping to almost 90 degrees for approach control. The LS-2's flaps continued over much of the span, with short, increased-chord ailerons. The Pik-20's flaps control is a hand crank with a rack-and-pinion drive that allows full lowering at any speed up to the red line in five turns. The Pik-20 was also the only non-white fiberglass sailplane. Since the early days, when it was feared that high temperatures under hot sun would cause too rapid a deterioration in fiberglass structures, airworthiness authorities demanded that such ships be white. Now that more experience with fiberglass has been gained, the Finns have decided that it is entirely safe to use yellow gel-coat, which improves visibility and recognition.

The instrument panels of championship sailplanes are always worth study. With cloud flying prohibited, blind-flying instruments were banned. George Moffat flew with a simple panel, merely leaving holes where forbidden instruments had been. Tom Beltz did not use even a basic speed ring on his variometer. Against this, the Pik-20 and other ships were fitted with air-data computers, and Hans-Werner Grosse had an integrating airspeed indicator. The rulemakers studied this interesting variety of equipment with care, but decided that there was no evidence that such sophisticated instrumentation would help a pilot to win. A somewhat different instrument, however, caused more concern—the Bohli compass. By an ingenious arrangement of gimbals, a bar magnet with a small red ball mounted on an extension stalk is capable of giving information on pitch and roll as well as direction. It would be hard to use this compass in cloud, but it would be perfectly possible to do so with training. Since cloud flying was prohibited, the best answer would have been to remove the compasses from the sailplanes so fitted; but the pilots had no others. Instead, it was ruled that the sailplanes concerned should carry sealed barographs as a check against cloud flying.

The organizers also produced some new equipment. One was a mirror sight device invented by Brian Lee for controlling sailplanes across the start line to ensure that they were below 1,000 meters above the ground and within the vertical "gate" limits. Usually, this is done by observers lying on their backs in the hot sun and staring at the sky—a method that is hard on the sunburn as well as on the eyes. Lee's invention allows the observer to sit in a normal position in the shade and look down into the mirror. Lines engraved on the mirror surface and reflected from a vertical transparent sheet show the gate limits clearly; the glider moves across the mirror without causing dazzle problems. The sight is rigidly fixed in a carefully surveyed position.

At Waikerie, there were only a few minor problems with photographic turnpoint evidence. The system used was based on that developed by the Soaring Society of America for the 1970 World Championships; the system makes it easy to take photographs of turnpoints from the correct places. Each sailplane carries two rigidly mounted Instamatic cameras aimed out the left side of the cockpit. Before flying, the pilot takes a control photograph of a board containing his competition number, the date, and task. On the flight, he photographs the turnpoints, and on landing he uses up the remainder of the twelve-exposure film roll with pictures of his contest number.

Soaring championships become more highly specialized each year, as performances improve and speeds increase. From places such as Texas and South Australia, 1,000-kilometer triangle flights are now possible; but to keep a lot of aircraft from outlanding more than a day's drive from base, weather forecasting of a high order of skill will be essential. The next championships, in 1976, will be held in Finland. This northern land of forest and lake will be a great change from the subtropics, but new challenges in new places are what most soaring competitors find attractive. The Finland championships should not lack customers.

9. Ballooning

A hot-air balloon consists of a 2-ton bubble of air heated to some 200 degrees or more, captive within a light fabric bag, from which is suspended a cab or gondola usually made of wicker, though some recent models are of metal or fiberglass. Between the bottom of the bag and the top of the basket, which are some 6 or 8 feet apart, is suspended a kind of metal table containing one or more burners. The burners are fed propane from cylinders carried within the gondola, and the flame is controlled by a valve—operated by someone in the gondola—located on the underside of the metal table.

Balloons first impress by their size. They arrive on a small trailer, the entire balloon and all its equipment squeezed into the gondola. When the balloon is removed from its canvas carrying bag and stretched out downwind of the gondola, it seems enormous—about 40 or 50 feet long. Then the mouth of the balloon is held open with sticks and the hands of crew members, and the burner flame is turned on and directed into it.

The 10-foot-long flame roars mightily and radiates enough heat to make you uncomfortable several feet away. The balloon immediately begins to swell, revealing a cavernous interior and billowing rapidly upward until it is the size of a small house. Crew members tug at cables and shroud lines, keeping the rim of the mouth away from the flame, and sometimes running inside the balloon to push and lift its rolling skin in the proper directions.

Soon the balloon is filled, and its underside begins to rise from the ground. The crewman handling the burner has one leg inside the gondola; at once all the others let go the lines and the bubble lifts, tipping the gondola

146

As dawn breaks, the balloonist and his crew are already at work. The balloon and gondola are laid out, awaiting the heated air that will give the bag shape and flight.

upright with the crewman inside. The burner is shut off. The balloon, inflated but still "heavy"—that is, not sufficiently buoyant to lift the gondola—stands now a good 40 or 50 feet high and 30 feet in diameter.

The passengers hoist themselves over the waist-high sides of the gondola and pull helmets down over their ears. There are several reasons for wearing the helmets: one is the possibility of a rough landing pulling everyone out pell-mell; another is the danger of the burner table hitting the passengers on the head during a moderately hard landing; yet another is simply to blunt the roar of the burners.

Everyone aboard, the pilot opens the burner valve; the flame shoots up with a great whoosh into the mouth of the balloon, which swells and distends; after half a minute, the gondola rocks slightly and drags a little along the ground. The burner is shut off.

The next step, you would think from *Up, Up and Away* and *Around the World in Eighty Days*, is for the balloon and its occupants to soar rapidly skyward, shrinking to a sun-sized spot and drifting off behind the hills. What happens is quite the opposite. With a delicate, magical levitation, the immense thing lifts itself a few inches above the turf and moves slowly away.

It is only a few minutes past dawn; the wind is nearly calm, there is still a slight chill in the air; except for the occasional chirp of birds, everything is still. Like a submarine moving slowly across the bottom of the sea, the balloon slides along—silent, level, graceful. In the gondola, the passengers converse quietly; their words are almost audible to the crew, who trail along behind the balloon, kicking the wet grass. From time to time, the pilot fires the burners for a few seconds, and then silence closes in again and the balloon is still floating eerily along.

The gondola is a heavy, sturdy wicker basket.

There isn't much room inside a gondola, and efficient loading of people, fuel, and refreshments is essential.

Propane-fed flame is applied, and the balloon begins to swell. Except for the dull roar of the burner, everything is still.

Two hundred yards off, the balloon settles with a little bounce to the ground. Passengers change, handing helmets and cameras back and forth.

When the new crew is aboard, the balloon ascends again, this time to 20 or 30 feet. It moves more rapidly now, passing through the tops of trees and skimming over a windmill and some power lines. The ex-passenger ground crew walks back to the car and sets off after the balloon.

In the gondola, one looks down from a small height at the fields and hedges below, and is suddenly aware of the life filling them. There are rabbits everywhere, which scamper frantically back and forth when the burner roars overhead. A cat prowls alongside a row of low bushes. A dog trots purposefully along a dirt road. Off a little behind the balloon, the ground crew is coming along the same road. Most of the farmhouses are still asleep, but occasionally, as a dog sets up a great yelping and tries to dig its way under a woodpile at the approach of the fiery monstrosity overhead, an old man or a small girl comes out on a doorstep and looks about for the cause of the excitement, never thinking to look overhead as the balloon flies now silently along.

The balloon drifts among low hills; the chase car, stymied, stops at a fence, hesitates, and then doubles back to look for another road. Because of a venturi effect, the balloon moves faster over ridges. The pilot aims just to scrape the bushes along the ridge, and the passengers lean against the back of the gondola in anticipation of the jolt which, if it were hard enough, could spill them all out onto the ground and leave the lightened balloon to travel on alone.

It is impossible to steer, or even to make the balloon revolve; the fortuitousness, isolation, and lack of control are much of the charm of balloon flying. With nonchalant egotism, the balloonist drifts off, indifferent to the world except as a sort of terrarium into which he peers curiously, while the ground crew, for the moment his serfs, follow doggedly after him. When fuel runs low, he looks for a place to land—preferably a valley, downwind of a screen of trees, but any clear spot of 50 yards' diameter will do in a

As the bag fills, things become a bit precarious, for now the wind wants to take bag, basket, and anything attached to them.

pinch—and, coming up to it, he opens first a small gate in the side of the balloon to let some hot air escape and steepen the descent. Then, when the landing is assured, a ripcord is pulled that detaches an entire panel of the bag and lets the bubble of hot air escape rapidly. As the balloon sinks, the burners are shut off and, time permitting, the fuel valve is closed and the lines emptied. The passengers brace themselves, knees slightly bent like parachutists' and hands gripping the sides of the basket, everyone subtly trying to be behind the others in order to land on top in the melee. The gondola hits and tips over; the balloon, deflating rapidly, falls beyond it. The passengers tumble into a heap like scrimmagers. As they pick themselves up and dust themselves off, curious passers-by arrive in pickups or afoot to ask questions—always the same, with a few surprising variations—and to gape at the huge collapsed balloon.

Shortly thereafter, the ground crew arrives in the car; the balloon is milked of its remaining hot air and stuffed any-which-way into its bag, which in turn is loaded with difficulty into the gondola. With one man at each corner—including, generally, some drafted local help—the whole affair is carried to the trailer, everyone piles into the car, and off to a pancake breakfast at some local diner.

Ballooning, even more than skydiving, involves much effort and preparation to produce a comparatively brief and delicate result. While it is possible to do it by oneself, it is much more practical to have three or four people along to help with the struggle at beginning and end. For those in the gondola, however, of all kinds of flying ballooning, as long as it lasts, is the most satisfying; it lulls the mind, brings a reflective, philosophic calm to the heart, and gives an intimate view of the world of birds, household gods, and low-flying ghosts.

Looking at ballooning from the outside in, however, is a poor second to being on the inside as pilot, passenger, or crew member. Here is a view from the inside:

" 'The Aerostat' (emphasizing the word carefully, so that the FSSman will get the point that while he may think this is an aircraft, a true connoisseur knows that it is not) 'is red, yellow and orange—and orange—with a black

Maltese cross on the top. Maltese. M-a-l-t-e-s-e. Yes. On the top. It is approximately 55 feet high from the top of the envelope to the bottom of the basket, and 36 feet in diameter.'

"Deke Sonnichsen is speaking—an unmelancholy Dane, in a phone booth at Tracy Airport, California; he is wearing a pink cowboy shirt, mauve cord jeans, and tooled black boots. The eight o'clock sun is starting to warm the ground, the folds in the hills to the west are full of chocolate shadows, the air is still, and I am about to take off on my first solo cross-country flight in a balloon.

"There have been several months of preparation for this event—quite unnecessarily, but more of that later. I had started off with Don Piccard in Los Angeles, flying three up in an AX-6 balloon in Perris Valley, just on the fringes of the March Air Force Base control zone. An AX-6 is a 66,000-cubic-foot hot-air balloon—60 or 70 feet high, 40 or 50 feet in diameter, with room in the basket for three people, several fuel tanks, and a small card table. We would foregather at dawn at a place called the Perris Trolley Museum, beside a collection of superseded machines, sniff the wind in all directions and toss handfuls of dust into the air to watch their drift, and then lay out the balloon. I was astounded the first time I saw it—a whale-like black affair with some orange panels, enormously long, unfurling endlessly from a sack. A black balloon conserves heat best, because it absorbs more solar radiation than a white or colored one. Properly designed, a black balloon might remain airborne of its own accord on a sunny day; one of the earlier Piccards had, in fact, experimented with such a balloon, and Don was toying with the idea as well.

"He would direct the inflation, shifting from place to place, preempting the critical jobs himself. He always brought a few helpers along—his daughter Liz, for one, and people who had become curious about balloons and were sucked all unwitting into work parties.

"You have perhaps heard of the Swiss Family Piccard. It contains a passel of Pauls—chemists, inventors (of the dumdum bullet, for instance), jurists, and educators; an Auguste and a Jean—identical twins, who designed the bathyscaphe Trieste, in which Auguste's son, Jacques, descended to the bottom of the Marianas Trench, establishing a depth record that will not be

High drama in the early morning, as the newly born balloon strains for flight—with or without passengers.

broken until someone goes down there with a shovel. Jean was Don's father; Jean's wife, Jeannette, piloted a balloon of Auguste and Jean's making to 57,579 feet in 1934, becoming the first woman in space, a claim allowed even by Valentina Tereshkova.

"Don himself is the maker of the best hot-air balloons available. They are 'racing balloons,' light in weight, with powerful burners; their gondolas are of wicker. The burners, varying in number depending on the size of the balloon, are mounted upon a load plate, which is attached to the suspension cables—eight of them on small balloons, twelve on larger ones—that support the gondola. Piccard is youthful, eccentric, a deadpan joker and something of a show-off, lean and gaunt-faced, with a lot of curly black hair. He is one of the world's great authorities on hot-air ballooning. He sells his machines throughout the world, and is consulted by foreign governments that are only now arriving at the point of extending their aeronautical legislation to include balloons.

"Piccard would inflate his big black balloon, propping its mouth open with bamboo poles, behind screens of trees; he would take his guests up for hops of a few hundred yards, then land and discharge them. Liz and I would then climb in, and we three would set off cross-country. There was a time when you could get a balloonist's license—unrestricted free balloon, what's more, including gas and hot air—for a smile and the asking at your local General Aviation District Office. Then the FAA noticed that there was some unlegislated virgin ground here to trample on, and they set up license requirements—six hours of flight, a written exam, and so on. The written exam is a weird affair consisting (if you want to try for unlimited free balloon) of thirty-four questions on pilot techniques that any fixed-wing computer pusher could handle, and sixteen on the care and feeding of gas balloons that nobody at all can handle. Piccard is rumored to have had a hand in the making of the exam, and if it's so, then a desire to prick the pride of others must have been among his motivations. Nobody passes the first time, nor did I. I took the hot-air written next, which was similar, with forty questions instead of fifty, answerable at the rate of better than one a minute. I had more luck this time.

"The technique of ballooning is not difficult. Inflation is mainly a matter of getting the balloon laid out properly, which in turn involves an elementary understanding of its not very complicated structure. It is much simpler, for instance, than packing a parachute. Once it is laid out, it is easily inflated—in calm conditions, at least—merely by aiming the burner into its 10-foot mouth and firing away. Flight consists of turning the burner on full blast for ten or twenty seconds from time to time. The problem is in the timing; after a burn with the balloon descending, for instance, you may have made it 'light'—that is, lighter than air—but it may continue to descend, seemingly unchecked, because the momentum of a couple of tons of balloon and air, mainly air, dissipates only slowly. One's tendency is to overcorrect, particularly in the last stages of a descent to a landing; the seasoned balloonist is distinguished by his fine appreciation of the interplay of buoyancy and momentum, and may be recognized by his craft's flat cruising and straight glides. The path of the novice, on the other hand, is erratically sinusoidal.

"Secured to the basket by cords or chains are the tools of the trade: a welder's sparker and a wrench. The latter is for fiddling with the propane connections while standing on the edge of the basket at, say, 7,000 feet and holding on to a suspension line with one hand—real hot-shot stuff; the former for relighting the pilot flame. The sparker somehow got left behind; Piccard came running after me, waving it and shouting, when I had over-corrected to 200 feet and my pilots were sputtering. It is some comfort in these cases to reflect that in the event of a total burner failure, the balloon becomes a parachute and descends no faster than your average paramedic with a heavy black valise and a torn gore or two. Ballooning schools like Sonnichsen's—as opposed to self-help programs, like Piccard's—let you solo on a tether, so that you don't have to fall so far.

"The only control in the balloon besides the burner valve is the rip panel. One of the gores of the balloon is held in place from the equator to the apex by Velcro tape, and may be pulled out by means of a line, releasing hot air. This is an irreversible process, and best practiced at very low altitudes. It is a standard part of landing procedure. The balloonist's landing mnemotechnic is BURP (Blow out the BUrner, pull out the Rip Panel); the last step—brace yourself, knees bent, and get ready for the load plate and passengers to fall on you—is instinctive and need not be remembered.

"I learned early that the up-up-and-away scene is strictly for songs. Piccard's balloon, an inverted eggplant the size of a small apartment house, would grow light upon its basket-bottom like a quivering helicopter, rise above the golden grass to a height of a few inches, float there and move very slowly off like a large sailing ship in a calm. It is not silent, but alternates between silence (tintinnabulation of birds, aeronauts speaking softly) and the roar of the burners (three of them, on an AX-6), which drowns everything. Normally, the burners are fired off intermittently to replenish the heat in the envelope, which is constantly dissipated through convection and radiation. Some Philistines set the pilot flames in their burners very high, and thus maintain heat and height without having to handle the valve all the time; but the beauty of it is in the silence between roars, when one has genuinely the sense of harnessing a bubble of air and floating without sound or power in defiance of gravity. How preternatural this must have seemed in the eighteenth century, when a man or a mass suspended in the air without visible support was an unheard-of thing! That slow rise and the unconcerned smiles of the aeronauts must have seemed things of another world.

"Piccard is a virtuoso of the protracted low-altitude cruise; he would slide along the tops of the grass, brushing tall weeds and descending into depressions by a cunning succession of burns, never varying his altitude: rising over ridges, brushing their tops, dragging through the leaves and slender branches of low bushes or trees, sometimes putting a foot over a hummock to surf down the other side. Balloonists must have a delicate instinct for wind; he would point out the subtle increase in groundspeed as the balloon crossed a ridge (venturi effect), and climb and descend to take advantage of conflicting winds, sometimes bringing himself back to his point of origin on a higher, opposite-moving conveyor of air. Mostly, however, the balloon would travel in more or less straight courses, or knight's moves, and would finally land miles from where it had taken off.

"All the while, the patient white bug of the chase car would trail below, sometimes coming up to dead ends that we could see from the air but would or could not communicate to the ground. The chase car—befuddled, creeping, awkward, by turns racing ahead of a cloud of dust along a straight section road and hesitating, stopping, turning and humping backward over rutted dirt roads that ended in unseen fences—is the flunky of aerostation, the straightman, a bungling Robin to Piccard's unearthly, drifting black Bat-Egg.

"When you land, there is a public-relations job to be done. Inevitably, you have descended into someone's field and stomped on his asafoetida. However nondescript and dessicated the patch into which you choose to descend, there is sure to be a farmer—hankering after a lawsuit—whose pickup can reach you before your load plate bruises stop smarting. You rush up, ask his name, tell yours, soft-soap him, tell him about the balloon and what a perfect day it is, what nice asafoetida he has, don't let him get a word in until he forgets what he came for and melts under your draft of warm feelings. People come from all around and always ask the same questions. You enlist their help in stowing the balloon in its bag, and the bag in the basket, and the basket in the chase car's trailer. The trick is to make a formerly enraged farmer sweat helping you out.

"The danger of doing any real damage is slight; the direction of the balloon's travel is practically random, but the place of its descent is quite controllable. Piccard carries considerable insurance, a lot of it against damage to livestock. Animals, particularly pigs, have been known to become terrified and rush madly against a wall, or hurt themselves in some similar way. That is one of the few distasteful things about ballooning.

"Wind is the balloon's horsepower; but the more of it there is, the harder it is to get the thing inflated in the first place. It is like an immense parachute, vastly difficult to control, and difficult to heat up when it is trying to depart horizontally, spinnaker-fashion, across the ground. We had an interesting launch at the Paris Air Show, where I ran into Piccard and naturally got enlisted. It was blowing 25 mph or so. A British team had tried to launch something huge—an AX-7 or -8—the day before, with disastrous results; Piccard, who is not without his adolescent qualities, was determined that we would get his balloon off this day, come hell or high water. He backed a car up against a taxiway curb so that it was well chocked, and made fast the bottom of the basket to the bumper with a thick rope. He handed a large switchblade to Madame Duvaleix, the wife of the purchaser of the balloon, with instructions to cut the rope when he hollered, 'Cut it!' Piccard, despite his Swiss descent, does not speak much French, and Mme Duvaleix had even less English; doubtless she was muttering to herself, 'Cut it, cut it,' throughout the entire stormy inflation, lest her phonetics fail her at the critical instant. Liz Piccard and I, as the most seasoned assistant aeronauts present, got to handle the mouth; others were delegated to hold down the sides and the apex of the balloon to steady it against the massive rolling movements induced by every wind shift.

"Picccard got his burner lit off and aimed into the mouth. It was hard to keep the mouth open in the wind, which kept lifting the underside of the balloon off the ground into the flame. If you tried to stand on the lower suspension cables, they lifted you right into the air. Liz and I finally got the predictable order to get inside; by lying inside the mouth of the balloon, beneath the burner flame, you can hold the mouth down pretty well, and you may even have your one hand free to cover your face. Piccard was getting quite a gleam in his eye, and the burner was going like blazes, when I noticed that it was becoming a trifle hot. In fact, the wind was blowing the flame very near my face, and I did not feel competent to blow back. I yelled at Don for a little while, pretty frantically, 'Stop it, stop it!' and when he ignored this, I panicked and rolled out of the balloon, figuring, to hell with it. When I got out, I saw Liz still rolling around inside, yelling something. Piccard was very busy. At this point, Mrs. Piccard, a veteran of a ghastly 4,000-foot fall in a burst gas balloon and no doubt years of difficult launches of all sorts, sailed in after her daughter. 'I can't let you go on with this!' she cried to Don, who stopped his burner long enough to scowl. Liz, with more spunk than discretion, broke free of her mother's arms and seized the side of the mouth. The atmosphere was that of a battlefield. The burner was on again; we had our legs inside the mouth and were looking the other way, the flame was roaring and waving from side to side, and half the holders-down were off their feet, being dragged back and forth by the great yellow and blue balloon, which had by now the bulk and temperament of three elephants in *musth*. Piccard began to yell: 'Get out, get out!' at us, meaning, I guess, that we should get clear of the mouth and let the balloon start to straighten up; but at this point, Mme Duvaleix, whose phonetics had failed her, mistook the *'Sortez!'* for *'Coupez!'* (an understandable error), and began hacking at the rope. The thing came loose, rather unexpectedly, I think, for Piccard, who found himself riding the tipped-over basket along the grass like a Roman charioteer, screaming, 'Run! Run! Lift! Carry!' at his enlistees, whose business it now was to run the basket—which contained Monsieur Duvaleix in a foetal position in the bottom—along beneath the balloon, letting the envelope rise vertically above it. If the balloon is allowed to drag the basket, it lies down flat on the ground and can never be fully inflated; if you run the basket along under it, however, keeping up with the wind, the balloon straightens up and fills rapidly. We all ran, panting, lifting, despairing; but the gondola became lighter and lighter, stumbled less and less as it struck the ground, bounced higher each time, and finally rose—suddenly a peaceful and proud windborne bubble—at a shallow angle into the air.

"I had the taste of blood in my mouth as I stopped running, and the smell of burned hair in my nostrils; Liz was lying on the ground crying behind me. Ahead, the balloon was rising serenely, making a good speed toward a lot of parked Russian airliners. Somewhere, a crowd of 200,000 people was completely failing to appreciate the miraculousness of what they were seeing. Two calm figures, regal and triumphant, waved from the basket; on the ground, we flunkies sat down and more or less wept.

"The gap between the riders of ballooning's waves of glory and those who tread water underneath is not usually so great as this, nor is the sport generally so violent. Most balloonists demur at more than 5 knots. Paris left many a singed sideburn; in a situation like this, Deke Sonnichsen later told me at the Reno Air Show, 'You fly no matter what.' Even if it involves shredding the balloon, breaking your neck, and incinerating your friends and relatives—none of which is, in a good stiff gale, that remote a possibility.

"Piccard was constantly away; he sold his balloons all over the world and went with them to train their purchasers; he participated in races and contests. He was to and from the frozen North testing his *Sam McGee*, the largest balloon ever inflated on the surface of the earth (the Echo Satellite balloons were larger)—1,000,000 cubic feet, with a nominal lifting capacity of 20,000 pounds: Piccard's Pantagruelian baby. Because the process of getting the rating with him seemed endless, I cast about for an alternative, and discovered that in Menlo Park, California, there is a school of aerostation run by the only FAA balloon designee west of Philadelphia, Deke Sonnichsen. For $450, he sells you a private license course of five days or so, and an eight-day commercial course for $700. I settled for the private, and drove up to Tracy, where he does his training, one autumn Friday. He met me at 10:30 P.M., at Tracy Airport, signaling through the darkness with a flashlight. We slept out in sleeping bags, and were up before dawn to lay out the balloons, two of them, the other piloted by Bev Galloway, a co-aeronaut of Deke's. We flew that Saturday, and I flew again on Monday on the end of a tether with Fred Dingler, Deke's assistant instructor; on Tuesday, I soloed.

"The solo flight was not eventful. I covered 7 miles in half an hour, a good trip, at 500 feet and 1,500 feet, and landed on a dirt road between two fields belonging to a friendly farmer near Vernales, California. The sensation of standing in a balloon basket, like that of hanging in a parachute harness, is obviously different from that of sitting in an airplane. There is little to obstruct vision, and one looks about from a solitary eminence upon a bright matutinal world, through crystalline air unmarred by Plexiglas. There are faint puffs of breeze on your cheek as you rise and descend; the top of your head is warm from the burner above you. You have a variometer and an altimeter, but eyes are enough to tell you if you are rising or descending. There is almost nothing to do—just a bit of burner now and again. You are not responsible for your direction: you go with the wind. Farm vehicles crept about below me; sometimes people waved. Cars stopped and pulled over to watch. I was hardly of the world; census-takers need not knock on my basket, nor revenooers ask whence I had my $450. I do not need any of you any more; I do not weigh anything—and what is human life, after all, but weight? I was ready for a chat with Neil Armstrong.

" 'A long-established tradition at the Daedalus School' (says Sonnich-sen's poop sheet) 'is that the new aeronauts are baptized using the ancient ritual and ceremony which involves wine and champagne.' Sure enough. The ancientness of the ritual is questionable, since balloons have been flown for less than 200 years, but ritual it is. Sonnichsen makes a kind of mud pie of your head from the dirt upon which you landed and the champagne you will drink, and christens you with an aerostatical cognomen; he christened me Enigma Springs: Enigma because I was a little enigmatic, he thought, and Springs because something had gone wrong with my camera at the most beautiful of moments on Saturday, as Bev Galloway's balloon rose from the gray dawn mist after ours. We sat down on the farm road, took off our shirts in the morning heat, and finished the champagne. We were all Leos, and our birth dates seven, fourteen, and twenty-one—a fine thought to bask in after a fairly idyllic first flight, in the hot sun, with champagne. One feels rather special after such a flight. How many other people have done this? This is breaking the surly bonds not only of earth, but of purpose as well. This is the ultimate trip into the random, the uncontrolled, the spectacularly pointless—it is aeronautical pyramid-building. Just call me Enigma. King Enigma."

Introduction

SOME hobbyists are crazier than others. They go further, are more extreme, invest more of themselves and their wealth and time in what they do. The ones who build entire houses single-handed or who erect 70-foot concrete boat hulls in their backyards or who design and build their own airplanes are among the worst. They have lost all sense of proportion; they have forgotten that a hobby is meant to be a diversion from the serious business of living; they have got it all backwards.

The amount of work involved in building a modern airplane or in restoring an antique one is beyond belief. Much of it is spent learning what not to do, since most people build only one airplane in a lifetime. Those who build several find their investment of time diminishing as they learn shortcuts. One way or another, however, the thousands of hours of effort represent a decisive barrier to all but a few hardy, or misguided, souls.

Because of the sheer size of the task, it is difficult to carry oneself through it on willpower or patience alone. One has to enjoy the work, to the point where the enjoyment eclipses worry over the remoteness of the goal.

Some of the work—cutting and fitting steel tubing for weldments, for instance, or detailing from blocks for metal ribs—is sheer drudgery. One returns to it daily with a feeling of depressed anxiety. Other jobs, like setting up metal frames in a jig and skinning them, are rather pleasant, and provide in a few hours the sense of having moved years ahead.

Whatever the sort of work, though, you have to get *some* kind of enjoyment from it. You have to enjoy doing things; people who were not brought up to understand the workings of machines, to be at home with them and to be able to fix them when they go wrong, will not get the pleasure from working on airplanes that they should. Airplanes, after all, are simply machines; whatever the high opinion of himself that a person might derive from his possession and use of an airplane, when the time comes to fix it, it is no more than an inert, often recalcitrant heap of metal or wood in need of plodding, systematic attention.

Aircraft work has to be of rather good quality, since life depends on the proper strength and operation of many parts. It does not have to be perfect, though there are some craftsmen who cannot stand to do less than perfect work and who are attracted to airplanes because the general level of quality is so high. Builders have been known to polish all their solid aluminum parts and then anodize them in a homemade tank, all for the sake of a peculiar, velvety, mottled finish which even manufactured parts rarely have. Nothing of the sort is necessary; what is necessary is to avoid giving trouble a place to start. This means simply making sure that metal parts are free of nicks and deep scratches, that everything is protected against corrosion, and that bearings and sliding parts have provision for inspection and lubrication. Good mechanical trueness is necessary because twists and kinks in airplane structures show up in twisted flying characteristics, and the flexing of the whole ensemble in flight can cause a binding of mechanisms that do not move freely in the first place.

The work of the homebuilder is somewhat different from that of the antiquer. The antiquer is seeking historical fidelity more or less seriously, and he is as likely to reject parts because of where they were made as for mechanical flaws. Absolute historical accuracy is not always obtainable, however; some airplanes used hardware and fittings which have passed from this world and which would be impractical or impossible to re-create. But so far as possible, the antiquer would like to restore things to their original state, at least on the outside, and, if feasible, throughout the airplane.

The deepest satisfactions for the craftsman, however, lie in the beauties of good work. A builder who does not take some pride in doing his work well, and who gets no pleasure from the look of a neat weld, of well-finished wood, tight fabric, or even something so simple as well-bucked rivet, misses the whole purpose of craftsmanship. Love of fine work is disappearing from this world, and part of the appeal of antique airplanes lies in the abundant opportunities they offer for old-fashioned quality—coat upon coat of hand-rubbed paint, fine leathers, polished brass and copper.

The best work is done without impatience, without awareness of time spent or of time remaining to be spent. The hours go by stealthily, unnoticed, without their usual rumblings and bumpings. It is well that they pass silently, because so many of them must go by between the moment when you first pick up a tool in ambition, and when you set the last one down in satisfaction. People who are interested in building airplanes often pass over the building itself in their minds, dismissing it as a necessary evil lying between the desire to fly and its fulfillment. It can hardly be so dismissed, any more than a thousand-mile walk could be dismissed as a mere delay separating the origin from the destination. For a long time, the building is everything; it would be a shame to close one's eyes to the pleasures of it.

10. Building It Oneself

HOMEMADE airplanes have somewhat the same attraction as custom cars, but with an added dimension of precariousness. In an airplane, though, form is subjugated to function in a way it never is in cars; the creation of an airplane is an act well down the road from decoration to art. Like a chess problem, it is a puzzle in which every step has its interlocking ramifications, in which imaginative foresight is richly rewarded and carelessness harshly punished.

There are close to 4,000 amateur-built airplanes in the United States, with many more on the way. Most of them are built following sets of plans purchased from the designer; a few are even designed by amateurs, and an increasing number are assembled from kits supplied by entrepreneurs in the field. The Federal Aviation Administration, which licenses homebuilt aircraft, requires that, for an airplane to qualify for an experimental-category certificate of airworthiness, the builder must have done 51 percent of the work of constructing it. This is a meaningless requirement but a handy one because it permits many builders to avoid making difficult parts (such as cowlings, canopies, and landing gears) by buying them from other builders who, once they have prepared the tooling for a difficult part, put it to work for a profit.

With the really difficult things done for you, building an airplane can be a relaxing weekend pastime—though it may take all the remaining

The heart of the building experience: watching the shell of an airplane begin to fill up a garage as well as one's spare time. The plane is covered with Clecos—specially designed clamps that hold sheets of metal together prior to riveting.

weekends of your life. There is an uncanny agreement among homebuilders that the average cost of a project is $3,000, and the length of time it takes to complete 3,000 man-hours. Practically nobody keeps complete books, however, and nobody has a time clock in his garage; the unanimity on this subject may well arise from imitation. Some homebuilts have been completed in six months; others have dragged on for ten years, and costs have in fact run all the way from $340 to $15,000. Taking the 3,000-hour figure as representative, however, you can see that an airplane is not a tiny undertaking; if you worked two hours a night five nights a week, it would take six years to build one.

There is a type of homebuilt for every personality: for the cerebral, introverted type, sailplanes; for swashbucklers, midget racers; for antiquarians, replicas of First World War biplanes and triplanes; for Aquarians, single-seat midget biplanes that compress into a jewel-like form, halfway between airplanes and models, the essence of sport flying. For the modestly ambitious traveler, there are economical two-seat designs; for the high-pressure business-man whose repose is tormented by dreams of haste, 200-mph airborne Ferraris; for henpecked husbands, single-seat runabouts; for borderline cases, aerial birdcages looking roughly like a Wright Flyer.

Old-fashioned construction methods—wood skeletons, welded-steel space frames, fabric cover—still dominate the field, but sheet aluminum is gaining fast. The advocates of the former techniques argue that they are familiar to most people, and that woodworking and welding equipment and services are available everywhere in the country. Sheet-metal work is, by comparison, an exotic and obscure art, but its supporters point to its cheapness and simplicity, and to the small number of steps between cutting metal and seeing a final product. Super-simple sheet-metal designs are becoming available, as is the know-how to execute them. Foreseeably, the day will come when the older techniques will be elevated to the level of exercises in obsolete handicrafts, like lutemaking or sailweaving.

Aircraft hardware is costly, but homebuilders have proved to be ingenious in adapting inexpensive automotive and marine components to airplanes. Recently, the Volkswagen engine in various forms has become a focus of much aeronautical attention; cheaply and readily available, easily

Homebuilding attracts many imaginative pilots who are sure they can produce the better design that lightplane enthusiasts desire.

serviced and sparing of gasoline, it adapts itself handily to aircraft installations. Some builders use stock VW engines; others try to bring them into line with standard aircraft-engineering practice by installing dual ignition systems and driveshaft thrust bearings. Several individuals and companies offer VW engines specially built for aircraft use, at prices running up to $1,100—as opposed to the off-the-shelf price of under $500 for the standard engine.

Chevrolet Corvair engines have also been modified for aircraft use, as well as marine outboards and an occasional water-cooled automobile engine. To date, however, the majority of homebuilts have been powered by conventional aircraft engines, of which the most generally available range in power from 65 to 250 horsepower.

Because of their small size and the special care that goes into their construction, homebuilts that are built for speed are often quite a bit faster than their industry counterparts. The record for miles-per-hour-per-horsepower at the moment goes to a Wittman Tailwind (a popular high-wing two-seat design) that cruises at 155 mph with a 90-hp engine; and honors for absolute speed go to midget racers—up to 260 mph on 140 hp or so—and to airplanes like the two-seat, fixed-gear Thorp T-18, some examples of which, powered by 200-hp Lycoming engines, attain speeds of nearly 220 mph.

The choice of an airplane is practically the choice of an engine, and vice versa; the engine is sure to be the most costly single item in the project, and the more ambitious the design and the more powerful its engine, the more painful the bill will become. An engine installation costing less that $1,000, all told, is a comparative rarity. Since used two-seaters—Cessna 120s and 140s and the like—can be had these days for $1,500 and up, it is evident that homebuilding is not the cheap way to get an airplane, just as it is certainly not the quick way.

The glorious impracticality of the homebuilder's impulse finds its loftiest expression in the convicts who built a Pitts Special biplane in a prison workshop—a projection of fantasies of flight—and the Los Angeles man who built a Smith Miniplane without knowing how to fly. Obviously, it is the building alone that rewards these men; and for many others, if the amusement of building is not altogether its own reward, it is at least a palliative for the frustration and boredom of a project that, like a runner in a nightmare, presses always onward and yet seems never nearer to its goal. Months are spent making individual parts and stacking them up in corners. Months more are spent assembling them into a recognizable airframe, and assuring one's self and one's friends that it will only be a few months more. Yet more months go to the installation of the engine, controls, and miscellaneous hardware—the part that seems simplest, and yet takes as long as the construction of the airframe. Still the job is not finished. Systems must be tested, adjustments and changes must be made, and fairings, trim, electrics—everything must be brought into good working order. Homebuilders have their variations on a standard joke about the estimated date of completion: "I expect to be done on Thursday." Which Thursday is not specified.

Eventually comes the day that is the best of times and the worst of times. The airplane is carted out to an airport, and then flight is staring you in the face. There is no longer time to see to this adjustment **or that** one, or to check cotter pins and safety wires once again; it has all been done twice, and there is nothing remaining to protect you from the ultimate duty.

One's concern is not alone for one's personal safety, but for the safety of the airplane, and for one's self-esteem and satisfaction. This last is worst: What if I don't enjoy it? What if it wasn't worth doing?

You taxi up and down, gradually increasing speed until you are making taxi runs at the edge of flying speed. At last, with an absurdly unreliable final cockpit check, you roll out to fly. It's just a hop the first time: wheels off the runway, check the controls—careful not to over-control, these homebuilts are light—and put it down again. Then you take off in earnest, and if you are lucky, it all explodes in your mind at once: the ground falling away, the tremulous levitation of small wings, the comfortable familiarity of the sensations of flight mixed with this one unfamiliar and dazzling sensation: I created this. It is a small renaissance of the self, just as at the moment of first solo, first parachute descent, first balloon ascension, first sailplane flight; a moment of exhilaration, curiosity, vanity, philosophy, compassion for the small figures following your flight from the ground below, and a startled uncertainty about one's own nature.

The FAA requires that the airplane be flown from fifty to seventy-five hours in a thinly populated area in order to demonstrate its airworthiness with a minimum of risk to innocent passers-beneath. After that, you have approximately the same rights as factory machinery, except that the particular nature of your mount entitles you to be self-congratulatory, smug, and boring beyond the levels usually reserved for the flying fraternity.

CHAPTER **11. Melmoth**

HOMEBUILT airplanes mature slowly out of old fantasies. Ones begun prematurely are apt to wither on the vine.

The extravagant project now called *Melmoth* was germinated more than ten years ago in a plan for a father-and-son team to fly two Piper Comanches around the world. The trip never materialized, but it set in motion in the mind of the son a scheme for building an airplane that would be capable, at the outset, of doing what the Comanches could do only with the help of auxiliary tanks: fly 3,000 miles without refueling. That figure represented the distance from California to Hawaii with a good reserve. The California-Hawaii leg is the longest one on a flight around the world, and being able to fly it came to represent a degree of personal mobility that would permit one to go anywhere in the world at his whim.

It was a long way, Peter Garrison discovered, from purpose to process, and a longer way still to realization. He made several starts on single-seat designs, proceeding at first crudely and childishly, later with an increasing familiarity with the quirks of aluminum sheet and the idiom of lightplane design. The idea was in his mind in 1963, but it was not until 1968, when he was living in London as an assistant editor of a small aviation magazine, that he put on paper the configuration that was eventually to be built: a side-by-side, two-seat airplane with a very small wing and a tell-tale resemblance to a World War II fighter—an airplane not mathematically optimized, but born of heroic fantasies and aesthetic cravings.

Garrison returned to his home city of Los Angeles in late 1968 with a

172

Two cars in every garage is no longer a dream, but for most people, two cars and an airplane in the backyard is still a fantasy. Not so for Peter Garrison.

sketchy design for the airplane and sufficiently definite ideas about its dimensions to begin building a few parts. He started with simple sheet-metal structures: the rudder, ailerons, anti-servo tab, and outer wing panels, which were to serve as fuel tanks holding 86 of the intended 146 gallons. He worked at first in a garage; then he moved and set up his shop in a semi-enclosed carport, into which the winter rains blew and on whose dirt floor delicate parts constantly dematerialized. There he completed the 12-foot-long double-slotted landing flap, the outer wing panels, and the big all-flying horizontal tail. After six months he moved again, this time installing his shop, with its drill press, rickety air compressor, bandsaw, and potpourri of hand tools of obscure origins into a former swimming pool cabana, which was dark and leaky but somewhat more watertight than his previous establishment. Here the fuselage took shape in the middle and end of 1970, and the elaborate wing center section, with its retractable undercarriage and Fowler flaps, went into the jigs in 1972.

The making of *Melmoth*'s wings involved many details, for the design was not simple. The outer wing panels (above) posed less of a problem and triumph than did the installation of the landing-gear-retraction system and the flaps.

The slowness and costliness of the process outstripped Garrison's most pessimistic forebodings. It seemed always clear that to make a certain group of parts, or to complete a certain assembly, could not take more than a day; but somehow by the end of that day, the work was always only a half or even a third done. Once committed to certain systems and structures, he was compelled to bow to whatever unexpected expenses might arise—and they sprang up like weeds. During his college years, his military service, and subsequent life in Europe, he had been extremely frugal; now he found himself like a company comptroller merely processing money which he would never see. He worked as an aviation writer, researching and composing his articles in the evenings and spending his days in his one-man factory. The project was a full-time one; and it was only because of the momentum of habit which it developed that he was able to stay at it for year after year. If the airplane had been in competition with his other concerns, he would never have finished it, because there were times of discouragement and depression when he stayed at the work only because he had no other work to turn to. The goal had long since disappeared from view; there was only a succession of small goals, things to finish today or tomorrow or by the end of the week, and towering expenses for goods and services which could be ignored because the money came and went as checks, and never, unlike his scant and precious European pennies, touched his hand or filled his pocket.

The expenses were high because Garrison chose, more or less unwittingly, the most complicated and expensive way of doing everything. The landing flaps could have been operated by an inexpensive electric motor and a fairly straightforward, reliable system of cables and pulleys; without too much difficulty his landing gear could have done the same; but because he found the problem of planning the paths of actuators in a confined space too awesome to approach, he instead decided to operate the gear and flaps hydraulically—a choice which later was to land him with a mare's nest of intricate lines and electrically operated valves, hundreds of dollars' worth of leftovers from the aerospace industry, and innumerable opportunities for failure or malfunction. He did not learn until much later the importance of simplicity and serviceability, or the fact that, tedious and confusing as complicated advance planning often is, it is still better to plan in advance than to put off trouble until tomorrow in the interest of peace today.

By the end of 1972, after four years of practically continuous full-time work, designing, and scrounging, the metal structure of the airplane was essentially finished. In 1972, Garrison found a good bargain in a used 210-hp engine that he bought and installed on his airframe, which now stood on homemade sawhorses in a clear space among the trees and sheds of his large, formerly rural backyard. A number of instruments were given him gratis by a man who had an airplane reconditioning business and who had read about Garrison's project in *Flying* Magazine. Despite the installation of engine, instruments, and airframe, however, the plane was very incomplete. It still needed a cowling, wing tip fuel tanks, windows, tip fairings for the tail surfaces, and a dozen other molded plastic parts before it could even fly.

At this point Garrison had a stroke of good luck. Just as he was beginning to tackle the difficult project of making molds for the cowling, a man named Karl Krumme showed up to do it for him. Krumme was a freelance auto body customizer and stylist, a talented exponent of the foam-and-Bondo school of the plastic arts, with a good eye and hand for smoothly flowing curves. He went to work on the cowling, tip tanks, and canopy molds, and in a few months all those difficult parts were made. Krumme cost Garrison a lot of money, but much of the visible beauty of the airplane is due to his work.

A good part of 1973 was spent in a seemingly endless process of wrapping things up. The airplane did not need to be finished in order to fly. It seemed in the spring that only a few odds and ends had to be seen to before there would be at least a flyable machine whose qualities could be assessed, and which might put an end to doubts about what Garrison, working more or less in aerodynamic darkness, had managed to create. The odds and ends, however, dragged on and on. In midsummer, Garrison fell while stepping down from the wing of the plane and broke his wrist. He was in a cast for six weeks, and worried that when the time came to fly the airplane, he would not be in shape to do it. But the cast came off in August—he had continued working with friends serving as left hands all the while—and by the beginning of September, the airplane was ready to fly.

The nervous system of an airplane is born first of inelegant open spaces where instruments and wiring should be. In the beginning (above), *Melmoth*'s cockpit seemed bare indeed, then cables and instruments were added and meshed (right). Even during its first flights (below) the cockpit seemed extremely anatomical.

Back in 1970, when he had written his first article on the then barely started project, Garrison had jokingly christened his creation *Melmoth*—a queer-sounding name which came from a nineteenth-century horror novel about a man who sold his soul to the Devil in return for, among other things, a preternatural ability to move about freely in space and time. John Melmoth brought disaster with him wherever he went, but Garrison was more interested in mobility. The name started off as a joke, since at the time it seemed quite unnecessary for the heap of aluminum scraps in the backyard to have any name at all. Later it took over, and everyone came to refer to the growing airplane as *Melmoth*. An imaginary company, Oneirodyne, was concocted to be the nominal manufacturer of *Melmoth*—the company's name was derived from the Greek words for "dream" and "power"—and the airplane was christened the Oneirodyne OM-1. Its registration number, 2MU, referred to a syllable meaning "nothing," used in meditation by Zen Buddhists somewhat as "Om" is used by Tibetan Buddhists.

The airplane, a patchwork of primer colors and mystical references, was loaded aboard a borrowed trailer and towed out to the desert north of Los

In the Los Angeles sun, surrounded by foliage and the flotsam of homebuilding, *Melmoth* awaited completion, clearly an airplane but an airplane still *manqué*.

Angeles for its maiden flight, flanked by huge hand-lettered signs pronouncing: "ONEIRODYNE."

The atmosphere was festive and fantastic. The airplane had so long been a flightless bird about whose airworthiness everyone was either secretly or publicly in doubt, that for it now to be going out to fly beggared imagination. Such times have a curious atmosphere for those intimate with them. Garrison was keyed up, he later wrote, but the sense of ultimate vindication or accomplishment which he had expected was absent. Perhaps its absence was due simply to his not being an emotional person. Faced with an opportunity for experiencing or showing emotion, he withdraws into a shell of detachment and perplexity. Another element in his detached reaction to the approaching moment of flight may have been fear. He knew that among the many possibilities surrounding a first flight, one was that he might be injured or killed. Rather than allow the imagination of disaster to swell in his mind, he put all fantasies and feelings aside, and concentrated, as he said, from moment to moment on what was before him then.

The airplane was trailered to Mojave on September 5 and quickly assembled. It was fueled, and then Garrison started the engine and taxied hesitantly around the ramp and out to the runway. He had talked before of approaching flight slowly, perhaps through several days of taxi tests, but now he moved rapidly ahead, and in a few minutes was making runs at high speed down the runway. Basic questions were answered immediately: the brakes and steering worked well, the engine did not overheat, and the landing gear did not collapse when *Melmoth* turned. It was late in the day, and the hidden tension was great. Rather than attempt a flight, he decided that it was enough to taxi that day, and that he would fly the next day.

The next morning, Garrison and his friends were back at Mojave. One of them, Howard Morland, was to fly in the right seat to observe, give comfort and advice, and keep Garrison company if things went ill. They made a number of runs up and down the 2-mile runway of the former air force base, accelerating, rotating, sometimes lifting off, settling back down, and braking heavily, then turning around in the calm morning air and repeating the process. They quickly wore out a set of brake discs and pucks this way, since the lack of wind made it possible to run back and forth along the runway, rather than making all the test runs in the same direction, so there was insufficient time between runs for the brakes to cool.

By midday, the plane had made several short hops off the ground. Garrison felt it was nose-heavy, a problem which was temporarily corrected by tying a steel oxygen cylinder into the tailcone. After this adjustment had been made, he and his friend climbed aboard, saying that they would make one more run up and down the runway, and then if all went well would assay a proper flight.

He knew already as he rolled out, though, that it was fifty-fifty to go on the first try. He performed his cockpit check with care, and then, as though he were in any other airplane, he taxied out onto the runway, pushed, and waited for the feel to come into the stick and the plane to grow light as it raced forward at a rapidly increasing speed.

At 80 knots the plane felt right, and he lifted it off. The balance was good now, and over the roar of the engine and the wind he yelled, "We're

Gleaming dully but whole, *Melmoth* stands ready for flight.

going!" to his companion and retracted the landing gear. The airplane surged upward, powerful and light, its altitude and speed increasing in pace with the swinging needles on the panel. Garrison's attention was riveted on the instruments, the sounds, the feel of the airplane. He was unaware of the people below, the parachute strapped to his back, the fact that this was what he had been working toward for five years and planning for ten. There was just noise, airspeed, altitude, the pleasant lightness of the ailerons, his friend alongside him looking curiously out at the desert below them—but no sense of towering accomplishment or pride.

The first flight was short; they climbed 3,000 feet, performed some basic maneuvers, lowered and reraised the landing gear, and cycled the flaps; and when these essential checks were completed, they looked at each other with slight smiles of relief at not being dead, and with a shrug and raised eyebrow that said, "So, it's just an airplane after all." Something was wrong with the propeller governor, and the engine speed was not as controllable as it should have been; rather than prolong the flight, Garrison turned back to the airport. They flew the pattern at high speed, leaving ample margins above stall, touched down at 80 knots, and rolled for 4,000 feet, coasting and enjoying it, before turning off the runway toward the little knot of figures on the ramp.

The expected congratulations were exchanged, Garrison said that it was enough for that day, and the airplane was rolled into the hangar and buttoned up for the night. The group of friends got into their respective planes and cars and departed for Los Angeles, 90 miles away. To be honest, Garrison later said, for all the fanfare about first flights and for all the work that leads up to them, this one really hadn't been much. The best part of it was that it was so anticlimactic—that *Melmoth* was an airplane like any other. He had not created a monster.

Test flights went on for more than a month, until the fifty hours required by the FAA had been accumulated and the airplane could be brought into the city. In mid-October *Melmoth* finally moved to an airport in Los Angeles, there to be partially disassembled for inspection, modification, and completion of parts that had been held together with tape and temporary

Test flight for *Melmoth*. Attached to the fuselage are tufts of material used in studying aerodynamic flow.

fasteners during the test flights. There was a lot to do, and it was two months before the plane flew again. The tests had revealed that there would be still more to do before Garrison got the kind of airplane he wanted.

Further flying through the winter confirmed what the initial tests had indicated: insufficient vertical tail area and a flow interference between the landing flap and the horizontal tail when the flap was lowered for landing. The two-birds-with-one-stone solution to this situation, which had the further advantage of falling in nicely with what is currently chic in aeronautical styling, was to enlarge the fin, beef up its structure, and mount the horizontal tail on top of it, where it would probably be above the wake of the wing flap. Doing this meant grounding the airplane for several weeks, so the modification was put off until a fiscally convenient moment arrived for the removal of the engine for overhaul, for which it had been about due when Garrison first bought it. When the engine came out the plane was grounded anyway; at this point, Garrison brutally chopped off the old tail assembly and built a new one. The whole operation took three months, the last few weeks consisting mainly of delays in completing the engine.

What rolled out of the hangar in May 1974 was in many ways a new airplane, and the second first flight was more exciting than the first. The initial configuration of the airplane had been completely conventional; the new one was less dependable, and there was a possibility that the flexibility of the slender vertical fin might cause a disastrous vibration at high speed. There was no way to know except by testing it in flight, but the tail's requirement of working slowly up toward cruising speed conflicted with the engine's demand that for proper break-in, it should be run hard, with the airplane at high speed, from the beginning.

Garrison approached this flight with more trepidation than the first

The dream flies. Straight and level, able to do what the designer wanted, *Melmoth* is a success. Its creator, Peter Garrison, is in the left seat of the cockpit, the position of command.

one, but, like the first, it turned out to be uneventful. The airplane flew as before, with only the desired changes brought about by the T-tail (though it was still not so directionally stiff as he would have liked). Performance disappointingly remained the same, with a cruising speed of about 190 mph; but handling in the landing configuration was much improved.

Now the testing went ahead rapidly. The speed envelope was opened up to an indicated airspeed of 240 mph; it was determined, for what it was worth, that the airplane was capable of looping and rolling, that its range would be at least 3,200 miles, that it could operate from 2,000-foot runways, and that it flew well hands off. Stalls, which Garrison had skirted before because of possible problems arising from the flap wake enveloping the horizontal and vertical tail, were now explored; there were no surprises.

The airplane made a number of long trips, including one from Los Angeles to New York, thence to Guatemala, and thence back to Los Angeles, when it was still unfinished. But gradually, the remaining work grew less and less, until it blended imperceptibly into the routine service which the airplane would continue to require as long as it flew. The project, which was probably more complicated and ambitious than any other homebuilt airplane had ever been, never really came to an end; like Manhattan, it was always being worked on.

Its successful realization was remarkable as a proof of the efficacy of a cookbook method for airplane design. Garrison had no background in aeronautical engineering; he had a college degree in English, and that was all. But everything he needed to know was to be found in any technical library, waiting to be converted from ink into aluminum. He probably had a tremendous advantage over most prospective homebuilders in the amount of free time he had at his disposal; he was able to make a full-time job of building the airplane, and could thus prevent discouragement by the sheer force of habit. It would seem from his example, though, that, given the time and the desire, anyone who could read and understand the fairly simple tests which Garrison used could design and build his dream and fly it where he liked—and unlike John Melmoth, he would not even have to sell his soul to the Devil in order to do so.

SECTION FIVE *Nostalgia*

Introduction

IT's hard not to have a fondness for any machines built long ago. They did things differently then, manufacture was profligate of labor, and old airplanes and cars and buildings betray a most unmodern callousness about the accumulation of man-hours. So much welding and woodwork, so many metal parts hammered, annealed, and smoothed, the hammer marks then erased by skillful and sensitive hands; so many little chips, stitches, and screws! And yet these old airplanes were assembled with phenomenal speed and at very low cost, perhaps because the notion of "aircraft quality" had not yet come into its own.

Not only were the old airplanes complicated and full of baffling idiosyncrasies, both of construction and of flying qualities, but they sprang up in incredible variety. It was with the old airplanes as with the old cars: companies came into being, built one, two, or a dozen planes, and then disappeared. Almost every builder had some characteristic peculiarity, a trademark of shape or a trick of construction, that marked his product. Experts can still pick them out today by name and year, where and how they were built, where they flew, and how they ended up.

Many of them are gone forever. Wood, fabric, and steel are perishable materials, and if the steel is the last to go, it still takes only a few years of dew and rain to rot a welded fuselage into worthlessness. A few of them were kept pristine from the beginning; a few more were rescued before they became basket cases, and with some repair and recovering again became flyable.

The dream of the antiquer is to peek through the doorway of an old barn somewhere, someday, on some other errand, and see, hanging from the rafters and covered with dust, the restorable ruin of some rare and memorable biplane. Many planes have been found in such a way, often in foreign countries, or in improbable corners of the Midwest; once found, they have been gobbled up sometimes at bargain prices by poker-faced restorers.

Restoration, even of an airplane in seemingly good condition, is a monumental task. The restorer begins by imagining that he will do just such and so; but when he proceeds to do so, he notices something else that needs attention; then, when he takes that item apart, he notices something else, and so on and so on, until the airplane is disassembled down to irreducible parts. When every part has been inspected, repaired, refinished, or replaced, the whole airplane is reassembled. Many antiquers have restored several airplanes, and when they have done one or two, they learn to despair of shortcuts. There is a fanaticism to serious restoring that will not suffer a hidden flaw. No self-respecting antiquer would put a beautiful finish on an airplane whose concealed interior contained rust or cracking wood or peeling varnish.

The mainspring of it all is usually vanity rather than a passion for historical accuracy. Fine antiques are generally in far better condition than the originals ever were, and they tend to be gussied up in ways uncharacteristic of the struggling but golden years of the biplane. Chrome-plated exhausts and fittings and cockpits of hand-tooled leather were not the rule on airplanes which landed in wet fields of tall grass and were boarded by muddy-shoed aviators and awkwardly clambering passengers. In reality, they were repaired with canvas patches and baling wire, their engines spat and spewed oil, their props had tips streaked with green from scything grass strips, and their engines and windshields were encrusted with squashed bugs.

The desirability of antiques may spring from several sources. For one, sheer rarity has its charm; if you can find an airplane of which only one has ever existed but of which many people have heard, you have a good item. On the other hand, familiar, fairly common types like the Tiger Moth and Stearman offer an opportunity to do one's fellow restorers one better. Some airplanes, like the Staggerwing Beech and Globe Swift (the latter is properly called a "classic" rather than an "antique," but its appeal to the restorer remains the same), have beautiful shapes which are appealing to anyone, and which make up for the relative commonness of the airplane. Others simply look unforgettably striking, like the Boeing P-26 or P-12; they are great attention-getters.

There has been some interest in building miniature copies of antique airplanes; World War I fighters are popular candidates for this treatment because so few of them are available for restoration. Usually the copies are of inferior detail quality. Another less common and more demanding course is to build a full-size replica of an airplane which no longer exists at all; one such is the new, nearly completed reconstruction of Ben Howard's famous racer *Mister Mulligan*. In this case, nothing but photographs of the airplane remained, along with the recollections of men who had seen it or worked on it; but it was a memorable airplane of phenomenal performance, which well deserved to be recreated. In such a case, the internal structure is not necessarily similar to that of the original, but the wooden frame supporting the fabric, which gives it its shape and contour, and all the externally visible structure, would be the same as the original's.

Apart from the challenges to patience and craftsmanship which a good restoration presents, old airplanes have a charm of their own, the reflection of a *Zeitgeist* different from our own and which we will never recover. They were built by men who were still seeking keys to the last recesses of flight, and who did not have the cynicism of modern designers. They took many shots in the dark; and the airplanes they produced reflect, more than any of the cookbook-and-committee airplanes of today, the instincts and impulses of their individual genius. Many of them are genuine curiosities—unique instances of features of design or structure subsequently superseded or discarded.

They also fly in ways more various and idiosyncratic than any modern machines. They sometimes, though not always, achieved remarkable performance, partly because of their large propellers and slow-turning engines, but partly because of good design—tricks which people still have trouble duplicating today. There were other tricks, however, which were unknown then and are commonplace today—tricks for stability, runway handling, stall and spin recovery, and so on, the ignorance of which cost many pilots life or limb when the antiques were new and still causes some damage or discomfiture today. Most of the antiques are open cockpit biplanes, slow and rickety; open cockpits are now generally a thing of the past, though a few builders are willing to restrict themselves to the speeds—80 mph or less—at which an open cockpit does not cause severe and constant discomfort. And so it is now a particular and private pleasure to go flying over the countryside in an airplane in which one could, as in the early MG series sports cars, hang one's elbow out over the side and catch the wind in one's hair. Business did not press the men who built and flew these old airplanes as it presses us today; to build, own, and fly them is to make a step, with one tentative foot at least, into another time and place.

12. The Venerables

An old airplane carries its past in its appearance and performance, a tangible presence for the pilot to welcome or contend with. Design compromises of earlier days are reflected in the sometimes curious behavior of the ship. This pilot has the past firmly in mind as he sings the sometimes dubious praises of the Tiger Moth:

"It is England, 1930. The RAF is looking for a new basic trainer. Captain Geoffrey de Havilland's Moth has become the most famous light airplane of all time and is making the good captain rich. The RAF is interested in the Moth, but there is a snag: they are not happy about the accessibility of the front cockpit. Service crews all wear parachutes as a matter of course, and getting into the front—or instructor's—cockpit of a regular Moth means clambering under the top wing and through a cat's cradle of bracing wires and struts, which is no mean feat on the ground if you are wearing a chute, and would be quite impractical if you had to bail out in the air.

" 'Can de Havilland do something about this?' the RAF asks, and de Havilland, with prospects of a large RAF order at stake, sets to. No abstruse calculations in any design office take place, though; instead, a regular Moth is dismantled in a small shed and jury-rigged as needed. First, they move the top wing forward 18 inches, then 4 inches more. Fine; you can now clamber in and out of the front cockpit even with a chute strapped to your derrière. But the center of gravity is now way behind the center of pressure; so all four wings are swept back 9 inches at the interplane struts. (Pencils fly furiously across the back of old envelopes; still not enough, is the verdict, so the upper

191

To fly a Tiger Moth is a joy, until you make a mistake. Then, your ham-fistedness will haunt you. The Moth sees to that.

wings are moved back 2 more inches, and to this day, the top wings of a Tiger have a hair more sweep than the lower set.)

"After the first few Tiger Moths have flown (old Geoffrey de Havilland collects bugs in his spare time, hence the name), it is found that sweepback has brought the lower wing tips too near the ground, and the interplane struts are shortened to raise them. This explains why the lower wings have more dihedral than the top set. Thus fitted, an already sweet-handling design is rendered still sweeter, for the increased dihedral and the wing sweep add much to the Moth's lateral stability, as well as vastly improving the pilot's view. Yet the machine is not completely easy to fly, and still manages to do an excellent job of magnifying many kinds of sloppiness in piloting techniques without allowing them to become dangerous.

"There are those who maintain that in many important respects, the Tiger is a dreadful airplane. As one RAF flight instructor of the 1930s noted: 'The shaking and juddering while ticking over, the dreadful aileron control,

Though painted in Royal Navy color, there is something quite right about landing a Moth amid trees and grass.

the effort required to put up an inverted formation, the difficulty in operating in any sort of wind; no brakes and the tailskid tearing up great chunks of grass field!' He might also have commented on the quite extraordinary draftiness of the cockpits, but being a rugged Englishman, he probably didn't even notice. Nevertheless, and regardless, the Tiger Moth was good enough to win the RAF's order, and in the end, almost 9,000 were built. From the mid-1930s until long after the end of the war, there can hardly have been one British or Commonwealth pilot who was not trained in the type. This was the airplane that taught Churchill's famous Few, who began with the Tiger before going on to the Miles Master or the AT-6 Harvard, and then the Spitfire.

"Maybe some 500 Tiger Moths survive. The design even has an FAA-type certificate, obtained by an English company named Rollasons, at Redhill Aerodrome, Surrey, that sold one to movie actor Cliff Robertson and thought it would be nice to get it licensed for him. The old Tiger is enjoying a wave of popularity in the United States at present, and entrepreneurs are busy importing them from Australia, England, and Canada. They were built all over the British Empire, but the commonest version you see is the Canadian Tiger, with a canopy over the open cockpits, mass balances on the elevators, wheel brakes, and a tailwheel instead of the classic grass-aerodrome skid.

"A regular Tiger Moth will do a neat loop, spin quickly and stop spinning quickly, too, and perform perhaps the finest hammerhead you ever saw. Snaps are forbidden, for they weaken the rudder kingpost. Roll the beast won't, thanks to Captain de Havilland's patent ailerons. He set out to conquer aileron yaw, and found that this was mostly caused by the greater drag of the downgoing aileron, so he geared things so that the downward movement was severely limited. Unhappily, it is the downgoing aileron that also causes most of the rolling movement. You can roll a Tiger, but there's no pleasure in it. 'Toc H' Turner-Hughes, who flew a modified Tiger Moth with Alan Cobham's prewar air circus and kept very tidy logs while about it, can show a record of 2,190 rolls performed, as well as 2,328 loops, 567 bunts (forward loops), 522 attempts at upward rolls, 40 inverted falling leaves and 5 outside loops, all done in 780 hours' flying. He survives hale and hearty to this day. His successor with the circus, Geoffrey Tyson, flew upside down in a Tiger all the way across the English Channel to mark the twenty-fifth anniversary of Blériot's more sedate crossing."

"Great heavens, the memories I have of learning to fly in a Tiger Moth! Bumping and rocking across the turf to the takeoff point, yawing left and right (you couldn't see a thing over the nose) so as not to run into the Duke of Edinburgh, who was also learning to fly at the same time (not in any old Tiger, but the most highly polished AT-6 the world has ever seen). My instructor was a mere slip of a girl who needed a whole heap of cushions to see over the Tiger's coaming. We talked as ever in Tigers at full bellow through speaking tubes connected to earphones, a system that dated from World War I and was called a 'gosport.' It was only one degree more effective than telepathy. I can still hear Miss Hughes's pretty, girlish voice, full of exasperation at my ineptitude, distorted like distant, emptying bathwater, gurgling through the tubes: '*No no no*—like *this*.' And she'd take hold of the controls and do it right. Flying a Tiger was so easy when she did it, so hard when I tried. Across the gulf of seventeen years, I can still hear her reciting the takeoff checks: 'F, fuel on and sufficient; H, harness tight and hatches closed; T, trim set and throttle tension nut tight. Oil pressure 30 pounds, compass unlocked, automatic wing slots open.' You climbed at 65 mph and glided at 65 mph—aerodrome wits said you cruised and stalled at 65, too, and it was hardly an exaggeration. Redline was 160 mph, and the day we tried an air start, we were up to 155 before the propeller would turn over. On the ground, it was chocks, fuel on, throttle set, and contact. If she didn't go straight off, you listened for the click of the magneto impulse device, and if it was asleep, you opened the cowling and bashed the magnetos with a rock or a spanner to free it. (The engine, de Havilland's own inverted four-in-line Gypsy Major, is perhaps the most reliable small aero engine anyone ever built. It has automatic carburetor heat, for one thing.) For ground handling, you picked up the tail, balanced half a ton of airplane on one shoulder, and pushed and heaved.

"This is an airplane of enormous character, and one in which it is hard to come to harm."

Affection for old airplanes is not simply a naïve desire to return to good old days that were not all that good, or even that old. Old airplanes represent much more than that: charming individuality of appearance; handling qualities that can test a pilot to the fullest; a challenge to a builder's patience and skill as well as to his devotion to the integrity of his goal.

For one pilot, at least, as we have seen, the thrill of a Tiger Moth is much the thrill of learning to fly in a demanding airplane that was part of a noble tradition. To another, the thrill in that plane lies in restoring one to fresh life. Richard King helps run an operation at Old Rhinebeck Aerodrome, in New York, devoted exclusively to keeping old airplanes, especially World War I airplanes, alive and well. In addition to restoring a Tiger Moth, he has restored two old Piper Cubs and a Waco 10. His crowning achievement was building a Sopwith Pup from scratch. Here is how he describes the experience:

" 'So you're going to build a World War I airplane, eh? It's what? Going to have the original castor-oil-lubricated rotary engine? Boy, you're really asking for it.'

"I must have gone through this routine hundreds of times during the three years it took me to get my Sopwith Pup replica into the air. But then, the typical homebuilder silently suffers this sort of lack of confidence, whatever he's building, be it a Sopwith or a Stits, whether his fascination is with World War I or Wittman Tailwinds.

"The rewards were more than worth the worry in my case, however. Picture yourself in the cockpit of a Sopwith single-seater, the brrp, brrp, brrp of the rotary engine in your ears as you cut the ignition on and off, the blue smoke and aroma of burnt castor oil wafting back through the cockpit, the same castor oil spattering in little droplets and streaming back on the windscreen and polished wooden cabane struts. You kick the rudder bar to the left and now, directly in front of you, there's a beautifully colored Fokker D.VII.

"You see the pilot of the Fokker turn and look over his shoulder at you. He pulls back on the control stick and claws upward. You follow, the Gs pressing you into your seat, but you have time to notice the green-streaked fuselage with its black iron crosses and a gaudy orange stripe on the turtledeck and elevators. Now his rudder flicks and he disappears below you. You do a renversement and fail to see the Fokker until he is coming at you directly from the side.

"A flight of fancy? Nope. On many a Sunday afternoon, you will find such a scene taking place in the skies over Rhinebeck, New York, home of Cole Palen's famous World War I aviation museum, the Old Rhinebeck Aerodrome. The Fokker D.VII belongs to and is flown by Baron Von Palen, and the Sopwith Pup is mine.

"Where do you find a flying World War I-type aircraft? Easy. You build it. There just aren't any aircraft of this vintage around, and if there were, the price tag would be out of the question for the average guy.

"I built my Sopwith from original factory drawings procured from the Hawker Siddeley Aircraft Company in England. It's powered by the original

Cole Palen's Old Rhinebeck Aerodrome—where "the war to end all wars" never ends.

Le Rhône 80-hp rotary engine, which is, in fact, a brand-new one. I found it in a small town in the foothills of the Adirondack Mountains, still in its original packing crate. The engine log shows four hours and fifty minutes of test-running time at the Union Switch and Signal Company's factory in Pennsylvania on September 8, 1918.

"I prepared myself for building this machine by reading books on welding and aircraft construction, neither of which I had ever done before. Anyone who tells you that building a real plane is just like building a model apparently doesn't know any more about it than I did. In fact, nothing could be farther from the truth. I never made any joints on any of my one-cent Megow kits like I made on my Pup. Never did I cut or burn my hands on a model as I did when filing and welding fittings and parts for the full-scale job. (My left hand was bandaged for three weeks once, after I grabbed a tube I had been welding and forgot it was the next thing to red-hot.)

"Probably the thing that suffered most during the three-year construction period was not my family (though certainly they paid a price) but the family car. From the moment I disassembled the back end of it so that I could load the Le Rhône engine aboard, it has been 'garaged' outdoors. Friends wonder what project I will tackle next, and the most obvious one is trying to restore the car. It costs about eight dollars an hour to fly the Pup, so buying a new car is out of the question.

"Since my motive was sheer enjoyment, I didn't attempt to keep track of the money or time spent. I only know that I cut the first pieces of tubing in May of 1964 and flew the Pup for the first time in May of 1967. It was most difficult to work on weekends when the weather was nice, since my home is only 500 yards from the Old Rhinebeck Aerodrome. On these weekends, Fleets, an Alliance Argo, Wacos, Fairchilds, Cubs, Champs, C-3s, and even an American Eagle crisscrossed the sky overhead; I had to force myself to stay in the garage and work. Even so, I could tell if it was a Kinner, Warner, OX5, or Le Blond as the aircraft made their landing patterns.

"Perhaps some of the finest moments of building an airplane come when you meet people with an interest that parallels your own. Some people come in person, some are helpful in locating parts and things, some—most—

BELOW AND OPPOSITE. Sopwith makings. Bit by bit, the old plane comes alive.

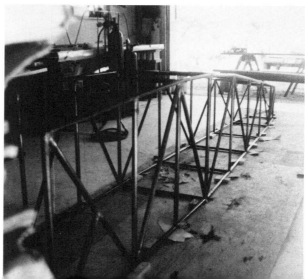

just happen to be people who have always wanted to do what you're doing but have never gotten around to it; they send their best wishes and want to be notified when you are going to fly it for the first time.

"When that moment of truth did come, Cole Palen had hopped it up and down the runway twice and had agreed that everything seemed to be in order; he was going to take it up for the first flight. Some people feel that they would want to be with their own ship on its maiden voyage, and, to be honest, so did I. But logically, Palen was the man to do it. After all, he's flown a Spad, Sopwith Snipe, Fokker D.VII, Nieuport 28, Avro 504, Blériot, Jenny, Waco, Gypsy Moth, Tiger Moth, Puss Moth, and a flock of other classics.

"The castor-oil tank was filled, the petrol tank topped, fire extinguisher made ready, and many of the people who had been sniffing around the aerodrome for the past few weeks anticipating the first flight were on hand. I was nervous enough that I asked some of my more experienced—and calmer—friends to walk around the airplane and examine fittings and connections to see if there was anything that I might have overlooked. One test eight of us (four under each lower wing panel) did make was to pick the entire aircraft up off the ground. Not a creak or groan was heard from the Pup. She was ready to go.

"We had planned to fly it about a half hour before sundown, because of the calm air, but a student pilot was just making his solo at that time, so they put off the flight until the student was finished. As luck would have it, the Le Rhône wouldn't start—the plugs were oiled. I drove into town to get some ether, a good castor-oil cutting agent. While I was gone, Cole got the engine started, but even though darkness was rapidly descending, he didn't have the heart to fly it until I returned. We started the engine again, held back on the wings while Palen made his cockpit check, and off he went. The Pup was off the ground in less than 150 feet, climbed about 1,000 feet per minute and, according to Cole, handled delightfully.

"The next morning, I was awake (if indeed I ever slept) and at the aerodrome very early. Cole flipped the propeller and the Le Rhône roared to life. I nervously made the cockpit check, which includes setting the pocketwatch that is bolted to the instrument panel (the gasoline gauge—you

Off she goes, into the blue yonder of Upstate New York.

know you have enough for three hours, flying time), checking the pulsometer
—a glass vial that has castor oil bubbling in it to show that you have oil
pressure, getting the proper mixture of 'spirits' and air so that the engine is
running smoothly and giving full rpm (which is 1,180), because trying to get
the proper mixture during takeoff could be disastrous.

"As I let the coupe button on the stick stay out and the Pup started
rolling, I felt a little frightened. I eased right rudder and a little back pressure
and floated off. I found myself really enjoying it.

"After about twenty minutes of just lazily flying in circles, I decided to
land . . . to try to land. All biplanes slow down rapidly when you throttle
back, and the Pup is no exception. When I started to blip the ignition to
descend, I found the glide angle to be quite steep. With the engine wide open

in level flight, the airspeed is well over 100 mph, but on touching down, the Pup stalls out on the peg at 30. However, it isn't necessary to look at the ASI, as the brace wires really talk to you. When it's ready to stall, they just stop talking.

"As I made my approach, I found that cutting the ignition in and out to control the rate of descent is not really difficult and, in fact, seems a quite reasonable procedure. With the steep glide angle, visibility is excellent. When you start your round-out, though, things get exciting. The nose cowling really gets in the way, and you find yourself looking from side to side in traditional biplane fashion. I made three landings, all on the same approach, and when she finally did stop, I found that the rollout was just over 100 feet."

There is a postscript to the Pup story. On the last day of the 1973 air show season at Old Rhinebeck, King accidentally ground-looped the airplane as he landed on the soft turf strip. The undercarriage and nose were damaged. King spent the winter repairing the airplane, a task that was made possible because he lives next door to the airfield. In fact, King, who is a teacher in a high school in Hyde Park, New York, discovered that he was spending more time at the field than at the school over the year and accordingly moved his home from Hyde Park to Rhinebeck. He is currently building a Royal Aircraft Factory BE-2C observation plane, another World War I machine.

A more recent airplane, but still an antique, is the Waco UPF-7. It, too, has the power to stimulate ardor in a pilot:

"When I was a kid hanging around the local dirt strip after the war (it was one of those hangarless boneyards populated largely by ex-GIs with more spare time than sense, as well as by at least one youngster eager to wash planes in exchange for rides—also with more extra hours than smarts), there was one airplane among that motley collection of surplus horrors that held my fascination. It wasn't the Bamboo Bomber that ran off the strip and wiped out its gear one windy afternoon; it wasn't the bright yellow PT-19 with the upside-down engine and strange roll-over pyramid between the cockpits; it wasn't any of the Cubs and Champs and it certainly wasn't a Waco, of which there weren't any on the field.

"It was a biplane, though—a big, ugly, oil-dripping stone of a Stearman that towered over my skinny, twelve-year-old frame like a mad monument to aerial daring. I always regretted never getting a ride in it, both because my parents forbade me ever to risk my reasonably promising future with any of the fools that flew out of that field and because nobody ever fired up the PT-17 unless there was sign-towing money up front.

"The sight and sound of that Stearman stayed with me, though, and made all the more meaningful my first look at Tony Barone's beautifully restored Waco UPF-7—a smaller, sleeker, more skillfully executed Stearman, if you will. The Barone family (Tony's father, mother, and younger brother and sister) runs a little airport and soaring center in what Manhattanites provincially refer to as 'Upstate New York'—at Wurtsboro, actually, about 70 miles from the city—and I first saw the pristine Waco after logging some soaring dual with young George Barone.

"'I want to show you something,' George said, and led me into the back of the main hangar. He lovingly lifted the covers off a tall, bi-winged shape and revealed one of the most delicate yet masculine-looking biplanes I'd ever seen—a blue and white assemblage of glistening stainless steel wires and hand-rubbed fabric, chrome in the right places and blunt black iron in the others, a carefully freehanded Waco trademark ('Ask Any Pilot') on the vertical fin.

"Some parents put aside a few bonds for their babies, or perhaps a tuition fund. Anthony Barone, however, stuck into the barn for his boys a pair of UPF-7s that he'd used during the war for cadet training under the CPT program. 'I know I enjoyed them when I was young,' he told me, 'and I figured someday the kids would, too.'

"The Waco model-designation system is one of those affairs seemingly meant to be crystal-clear to those already in the know and incomprehensible to outsiders. Almost all Wacos are designated by three letters, often followed by a number: UPF-7, YMF-5, QCF-2, AVN-8, and so on. The first letter

George Barone's Waco UPF-7—"one of the most delicate yet masculine-looking biplanes I'd ever seen."

identifies the make and horsepower of the engine (U stands for Continental 210s and 220s; V for Continental 240s; M for Menascos; and Y, Z, and A for various Jacobs radials). The second letter identifies the wing design and the third the model type. The dash numbers denote the model refinements; that is, there were F models -1 through -6 before the UPF-7 came along. And, by the way, the name is pronounced 'Whock-oh,' not 'Wayco' or 'Whack-oh.'

"The first F model—a designation that seems to have covered two cockpit biplanes with room for two in the front hole and one in the rear—came out in 1930, and it wasn't until 1937 that Waco got to the F-7. Production continued through 1939, and the entire 1940–42 run of UPF-7s went to the military—600 for the CPT program and 14 to the Air Corps for assessment as primary trainers.

"Waco, unfortunately, was in the same position as Ryan, which also attempted—largely unsuccessfully—to convert a sportplane (the ST) into a military trainer (the PT-22). The Stearman/Boeing PT-17 was designed for the Air Corps, and was made larger, heavier, and more rugged. It had narrower gear, to educate future fighter pilots, and therefore sat higher off the ground; it also had a thicker wing and more wing area, being in fact bigger and bulkier all around, although it used the same 220-hp Continental radial that the UPF-7 had.

"Though this combination of beef and brawn may have put Waco out in the cold as far as the Air Corps was concerned, it left the UPF-7 with a certain fineness of line, a combination of elegance and swash that the Stearman will never have.

"Since his ship hadn't flown since 1947 (and wouldn't again until 1967), Barone had to start just about at the beginning when the restoration project got under way in 1957. Besides brother George's airframe, there was a third UPF-7 stashed in the hangar rafters ready to be cannibalized for parts, so N30113 was disassembled, stripped of its skin, and painstakingly rebuilt from the inside out, using the hangar queen's contributions wherever necessary.

"The Barones are quick to give Tony almost all the credit, but everybody including his sister pitched in on the drudgework—the rib-stitching and paint-rubbing, especially. Why eleven years of work with such a crew, then? 'If you're working on a plane that isn't making you money,' explained pragmatist George Barone, 'you have to do it in fits and starts—when somebody isn't screaming for an annual, when your towplane doesn't need an oil change, when you don't have a student waiting. And eleven years of work did help spread out the cost of the job'—spread it out so well, in fact, that the Barones really don't have any idea of how much time or money they put into it. (A $10,000 offer for the plane after it won the best-restoration trophy at the 1968 Reading Air Show was turned down.)

" 'It also helped us turn out a much better final product,' George continued, 'because we never had any feeling of "Let's hurry up and get it finished so we can fly it." After a few years of work, you begin to forget about that.'

"The most visible deviations from stock, when you stand back and look at the Waco, are the wheel pants and prop spinner—neither of which were factory-supplied for UPF-7s—lengthened and chromed exhaust stacks, and stainless steel rigging wires (the originals were just steel). The pants were put on to keep the tires from flinging pebbles up at the wing fabric, but they improve the plane's appearance as well. They're a set that the Barones had sitting around the shop for years, perhaps from a cabin Waco, but nobody's really sure what originally wore them. The tires they clothe are from an Ero Commander, so that shouldn't create any availability problems for a while.

"The exhaust stacks were lengthened simply because the originals issued inches from the carburetor, and this gave UPF-7s a thrilling propensity for carburetor blazes whenever an overprimed engine backfired. An extra 4 inches puts the stack tips well below the carb. (Many Waco owners take the easy way out and fit a single-sidestack collector ring from a Stearman, but they lose the lovely, rumbling twin-pipe sound of the UPF-7.)

"Various other bits of updating went on under the surface as well. Wacos had a way of leaking gas from their wing tanks, because the internal baffles were riveted—not welded—to the tank skin. The rivet seals soon vibrated loose and, since the tanks are in the upper wing, the pilot found himself with a fine faceful of 80-octane during run-up. Barone's straightforward solution to this was to remove both tanks (25 gallons each) and completely fiberglass the exteriors.

"Projecting down from each of the tanks is a 6-inch plastic tube with a small red marker ball actuated by an in-tank float—highly dependable and simple gas gauges. The tanks originally fed the engine through solid aluminum tubing, but this was replaced by armored Aeroquip lines.

"The engine was entirely rebuilt, most of it by the Barones, and painted or chrome-plated before reassembly—accessory sections, electrical components, fuel and oil piping all individual colors, giving the engine compartment an exceedingly professional look. Still in evidence is a reed-type voltage regulator (within which a rocker bar consecutively closes one after another of a series of small, reedlike points as power demands rise), though conversion to a less authentic modern unit would probably have been easy enough. There's also a big, heavy-duty booster coil to aid in hand-cranking the engine. (We fired it up several times, both by hand and battery—neither presented any problems, provided you have a pair of nice thick gloves with which to handle that sharp metal prop. Proper procedure is to always turn it by hand a few times to spit out through the exhaust pipe the oil that has drained into the bottom cylinders. If enough collects on the wrong side of the piston and you do try to light it, you'll get a lovely hydraulic lock and a bent connecting rod.)

"Well, how does the Waco fly? George Barone took the back seat and I clambered up front. Visibility from the back, at least on takeoff, is atrocious, but up front it's impossible. Just to better the odds, Barone has a pile of little pillows in back that would do justice to your great-aunt's parlor.

"Starting up is straightforward, except that the starter motor is actuated by a foot button just like a car's dimmer switch.

"Another automotive touch is the trim crank in the rear cockpit, obviously supplied by the same house that made the window-winders for 1939 Fords.

"Needless to say, the engine, once lit, makes a fine racket—rather like a fleet of unmuffled tractors, but nice. We rumbled out to the south end of Wurtsboro's paved runway and did a simple run-up at what seemed to be about 1,800 rpm (the elderly tach needle in front of me wasn't all that sure of itself). I had time to note how really roomy the front pit is—the bench seat is intended for two—before George shouted, 'All set?'

"With a thunderous roar, the old bird tossed its tail around onto the asphalt and began a ponderous roll. The Waco is blessed with nonsteerable tailwheel, and directional control on the ground is largely dependent on the brakes. They therefore get a lot of use they're not entirely up to, and are prone to wear out quickly. Proper crosswind technique in the -7 is to hold the center-locked tailwheel on the ground as long as possible, not lifting the tail until you're sure of aerodynamic rudder control.

"We were off quite quickly, nevertheless—a good thing, since I have a feeling that the only things visible from the back seat were the south end of my head and the edges of the runway. We climbed out smartly enough, with a roar that diminished little during the entire flight; officially, one climbs at 1,800 rpm, cruises at 1,750, and takes off at whatever full throttle offers (the engine is rated for max hp at 2,075).

"One thing that intrigued me—having previously flown open cockpit only in aircraft with bubble canopies or long Plexiglas greenhouses—was the complete absence of wind in the cockpit. It was eminently comfortable, and I'm sure I could have spread out a mess of approach plates and area charts far more easily than in a Cessna with the cabin air vent pointed in the wrong direction.

"I wiggled the stick and rudders around a bit once we got to altitude and enjoyed myself by simply recalling that, twenty years after seeing my first Stearman, I'd finally made it into an open cockpit biplane. It did give me time, however, to get an idea of how light the UPF-7's aileron control is; unusual among biplanes of its day, it had both upper and lower wing sets of ailerons, linked by a hollow strut just aft of the N-struts.

"We full-throttled it for a bit, which certainly sounded very vigorous; the UPF-7 is said to fly a good 13 knots faster than the more obese Stearman, and 113, with its wheel pants, spinner, and highly polished enamel finish—plus the full cowling, which was off the plane when I flew it—ought to do as well.

"After a bit of simply messing about to no great effect, I turned around and made vigorous motions to George, at which point he cleared the area and pulled us heavenward—in an open cockpit, that seems to be the appropriate description—into a power-on stall. That one fell off ineffectually into a wingover, but the next one took us into a lovely spin, and a spin seen from an open cockpit, framed by a maze of struts and wings and wires, is a sight to behold. From the back seat, lord knows, it must be even better.

"We cavorted a while longer in the evening air, the Catskill farmland revolving slowly beneath us. Soon it was time to go home, and I remember looking over the side as we soughed along our base leg, sinking easily, the prop swishing along at idle; there right below me on the highway was a state police Ford, its red light spinning briskly as it sat behind the Mustang of a speeder, the trooper evidently writing out a ticket. 'Poor sap,' I thought to myself, 'he could be having so much more fun up here . . .'

"Make no mistake: landing an airplane like this is no 'drive it down to the ground' affair. Barone was evidently working a fair amount from the back seat, judging by the stick and pedal movements in my cockpit, as he brought it over the fence. The Waco is an especial handful in a crosswind, for the gear is wider than, say, a Stearman's, and though this adds a little stability, it puts the plane closer to the ground. If a wing begins to drop in a crosswind once you've touched down, you've got to feed in opposite aileron without wasting a second, for that control correction will put the downwind aileron even closer to the ground. If it hits, it may make inevitable that incipient groundloop. (Next time you see a UPF-7, take a look at the wrinkles in its lower ailerons.)

"When the whole world turns to the whistle of turbines, though, and flying is a matter of hands-off this and automatic that, when the fabric rots through and the round engine barks its last, it's nice to know that somewhere, someone will be waiting to bring it all back and face afresh the sometimes pointless, sometimes valuable challenges of basic aviating."

CHAPTER **13. Warbirds**

FROM a pilot's point of view, the leftover fighters of the Second World War represent a combination of sophistication and availability which few other old airplanes do. Their enormous engines give them thrilling performance. From the standpoint of efficient transportation, however, they are not hard to beat. No warbird gives as many seat-miles per gallon as a good light twin, and its speed advantage is found only at high-power settings at which its range is impractically small. While people may tell themselves and others that their new Mustang is a fine transportation airplane, more likely its value for them actually resides elsewhere.

It's the sheer size of the things that counts. That and their forms speak eloquently of war or war movies to their owners and admirers. They are altogether masculine airplanes; they are the only sorts of airplanes that can be dived at 400 miles an hour or more, pulled up into immense loops with crushing G-forces, climbed at 4,000 feet a minute, and whose engines start up with clouds of smoke that in another sort of airplane would send ground crews scurrying for their fire bottles. They are airplanes of extremes, with many-armed monster propellers towing swollen fuselages with steps carved in the sides for climbing aboard; they have hard wings you can walk on from end to end, blunt stubs of machine guns, and notices of caution and danger in a firm military font.

Many of the men who fly them are below fifty years of age and therefore cannot have flown them in the war. Their fondness for the airplanes is based not on rekindled memories but on the aura exuded by those planes, an

210

aura which an aeronautically inclined boy could pick up in the forties and fifties from magazines or from the model planes he built. They have a quality of virile pomp and force, undiluted by considerations of cost or comfort; at rest, they have the air of some professional fighter or killer at his leisure, now gentle but full of awful possibilities.

In flight, they handle well, though some are better than others. They are as a rule responsive to the controls; stick forces are light to moderate. The pilot must be mindful of the big engines and props at low speeds, especially during takeoff; too rapid an application of power during takeoff can pull certain fighters straight off the runway despite all the right rudder the pilot has to offer, or roll them inverted in a sudden go-around. They are usually landed on the main wheels, rather than mains and tail or "three point," though their runway handling is not excessively difficult to master—they were, after all, designed to be flown by comparatively low-time pilots. Three types, the Lockheed P-38 Lightning, the twin-boom "fork-tailed devil" that flew in both theaters in World War II, and the Bell P-39 and P-63 Airacobra and Kingcobra, are relatively hard to come by.

The most commonly available types of surplus fighters are the North American P-51 Mustang, the Grumman F8F Bearcat, and the Douglas B-26, which is actually a light bomber and ground attack aircraft rather than a fighter. On the larger side, there are a lot of B-25 Mitchells around. Regrettably rare are the big Republic P-47 Thunderbolt, the very flyable Curtiss P-40 (like the P-39, notoriously inferior to the Japanese Zero but a pilot's airplane still), the elegant British Spitfire, the Chance-Vought F4U Corsair with its uniquely cranked wing, and the German Focke-Wulf 190 and Messerschmitt 109.

Interest in old fighters is increasing and their prices are consequently rising rapidly; as the money grows, the supply of airplanes grows as well. Many American fighters were sold to South American and Central American countries after World War II and they are now being bought back by American individuals and groups such as the Texas-based Confederate Air Force, which has the largest stable of ex-fighters anywhere. The jet trainers and fighters of the Korean period are beginning to be available, brought back from Canada by a California firm called Fighter Imports.

At the same time, several groups offer plans and kits of scaled-down fighters. The problems of scaling down are considerable since they did not have much fat on them to start with, and certain parts of the airplane, such as the pilot, have to stay the same size. The liquid-cooled airplanes like the Mustang and Spitfire present the problem of a slender nose which, when reduced to two-thirds or three-fifths scale, is too small to accommodate any suitable engine. The radial engine types, with their more spacious cowlings, are handier; and one California firm, which candidly calls itself WAR (for War Aircraft Replicas), offers kits for miniature fighters with Volkswagen engines. Their first prototype is a "standoff scale" Focke-Wulf 190 (meaning that the parts of the airplane are not in strict scale relation to another, but the replica looks almost exactly like the original to the average observer) with a phenomenal fidelity to the original airplane.

It remains to be seen whether the kits will satisfy the cravings of their purchasers. To someone who has never flown a fighter but has always longed to, the fighter *is* its looks, and the replica promises the fulfillment of a long-cherished dream. It may be, however, that the look will shrivel into unimportance in the light of the performance of the replica, which will be sleepy compared with that of even the most anemic and ill-tuned fighter with several cylinders shot off. Perhaps the replicas will reveal that the looks of the fighters are only a symbol to their admirers, a symbol of power—power in every sense, literal and metaphorical—and that without that power the looks are hollow. The original fighters may continue to be what they have been up to now: the real thing, the rare vintage wine, for which no substitute can be made or found.

In 1939, the British Admiralty issued specifications for a new two-seat fighter. The British were so tied to the idea of carrier aircraft serving a secondary but important role as anti-submarine aircraft that they found it impossible to conceive of a fighter without an ASW capability. In the absence of any navigational aids on board—British military aircraft were not fitted with so much as a radio compass until the 1950s—carrying a navigator was regarded as essential to get carrier-based aircraft back to their ships. Besides, two pairs of eyes were 100 percent better than one pair for airborne surveillance. For the British, the second seat was sacrosanct, and the two-man Fairey Firefly, which soon evolved into a prototype (a mock-up, really), was approved. Production began immediately, and the first example was delivered on March 4, 1943.

The Firefly had a rather undistinguished career in World War II. History says it participated in the campaign that led ultimately to the destruction of the German battleship *Tirpitz*, but its participation was said to be limited to reconnaissance. It was soon recognized as a strike aircraft of merit, however, and Firefly squadrons were successful in accomplishing significant raids against enemy refineries and shore installations in the Indian Ocean. Later versions served with distinction in Korea; still later, it evolved into a pure anti-submarine weapon, its cannons traded for sonobuoys but its observer still riding behind the pilot, faithfully watching the waters around England for the shadow of a hull or the tell-tale streak of a snorkel.

Although the Firefly failed to achieve as glorious a battle record as other, better-known airplanes, it established itself as a worthy design on the basis of longevity alone. Descriptions of it always begin with the admonition that the Firefly is to be respected for its twenty-five years of service to its country. This it did achieve, but it was not so much this record as the plane's overall handsome lines and striking appearance that have made it the favorite of Canadian Warplanes Heritage, Inc., which found a Firefly A.S. 6 in a field in Georgia and restored it to Mk. 5 colors and markings.

It is an immense airplane, one that totally dominates the group's home field at Hamilton, Ontario. Consistent with the aims of the foundation, Heritage's airplanes are meant to fly, not to sit in museums. Luckily, the Firefly, when it was found, had only 670 hours on the airframe and 60 hours on the engine.

With the Mk. 4, the Firefly's oil cooler was moved from the chin to the wing roots, as it is on CF-BDH. The resultant nose configuration recalls the Spitfire, an impression that is enhanced by the semi-elliptical wing, which had its tip clipped when the oil cooler was moved in order to keep the same wing area. A somewhat awkward extension of the vertical fin was necessitated by longitudinal-stability requirements. Not that the Firefly is stable.

"These machines were never intended to have inherent stability like

The Heritage Fairey Firefly, with wings folded, perfectly restored to be more than a museum piece.

Firefly on a fly-by, with its Youngman flaps extended in "cruise" position.

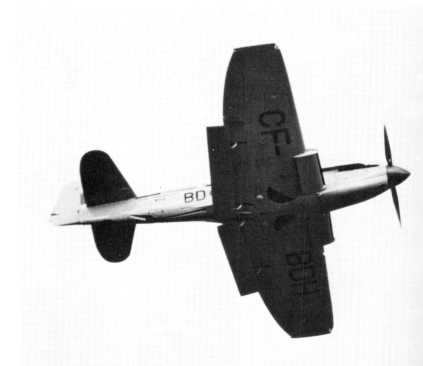

that found in the average lightplane," says pilot and Heritage partner Kennis Bradley. "It is this characteristic that makes the Firefly, even with its enormous weight and size, a joy to handle."

Part of the joy in handling this airplane is in deploying the Youngman flaps, which, unlike conventional flap systems, can be extended in two ways: at an angle, like conventional flaps, to produce drag for landings; or parallel, to the so-called cruise position, to increase wing area and effectively provide enhanced maneuverability. The idea behind the Youngman flap was to allow the pilot to increase wing area by deploying the flap into the cruise position: 3 degrees of incidence and with the flap chord line roughly parallel to that of the wing. Once deployed, effective wing area was raised and wing loading lessened. When no longer needed, the flaps could be "housed" and add no drag; it was one of the earliest and cleverest variable geometry arrangements.

A walk around a parked Firefly with wings folded reveals the intricate wing-locking mechanism that was mandated by the Youngman flap linkages, the pushrod (not cable) control connectors, and the sheer weight of the airplane. Luckily, CF-BDH has power wing-folding, sparing Hamilton's crew that heavy task. The Firefly's wings rotate about their hinges when they fold, so that they end up parked flat against the sides of the airplane, trailing edge down. When they unfold, they pronate as they swing forward. The locking pins are inch-thick, precisely machined slugs of steel that would look quite at home in a bank vault door. To lock the wings, CF-BDH has a manual lever that swings forward until it aligns with the wing chord to indicate that all the pins are home; the lever stows neatly by telescoping into the wing root adjacent to the oil-cooler ducts.

The A.S. 6 has the more powerful 2,250-hp Griffon 74 that was introduced on the Mk. 4. Along with the aerodynamic advantages that were incorporated, beginning with the revision of the oil-cooler layout, the engine's greater output improved the Firefly's top speed to 386 mph at 14,000 feet. Bradley flies the airplane in more gingerly fashion, ever mindful of the need to preserve the rare engine. He says he has never approached the 66 inches of manifold pressure available from the two-stage supercharger at full power. The Griffon turns a giant Dowty Rotol four-blade prop that is 14 feet in diameter. The prop turns counterclockwise, meaning that Bradley must have a strong left leg.

Fairey devised a unique jigging system for the construction of the Firefly. The fuselage was constructed in two halves, joined at the centerline. The semi-monocoque design had no stringers, relying instead on the structural strength provided by half-bulkheads and stressed skin. Fairey also incorporated a quick-engine change assembly in the Firefly, which became one of the first British airplanes to have what was then called the "power egg."

Although the Heritage airplane lacks the four Hispano cannons that would fully restore it to Mk. 5 authenticity, Bradley says the guns are ready for installation and will be in place soon. The only outward difference between the A.S. 6 and the Mk. 5 is the cannon; all other mechanicals are the same, says Bradley. The A.S. 6 is described as being outfitted with British sonobuoys (the Mk. 5 used an American model) that were carried in shrouded wing racks. CF-BDH shed these in the conversion to Mk. 5 equipment.

Part of the two-hour preflight Bradley conducts is taken up with charging the braking system to 400 psi with nitrogen. The Griffon starts eagerly and with comparatively little show of oil combustion. After warmup and run-up are accomplished, the flaps are deployed to an angled-down takeoff position that varies with loading. The tailwheel is locked once the Firefly has taxied to takeoff position, and the tail is held down firmly so that the locked wheel can help the pilot fight the engine's frightful torque. At 55 knots, the rudder takes over and the tail can be lifted; rotation comes at 90 knots. Boost is reduced from the takeoff value of 8 to 10 pounds to about 4 pounds, and rpms are reduced from their maximum 2,750 to about 2,400. Bradley babies the climb at a mere 1,500 fpm.

Besides the pushrod control feet that make Bradley's eyes light up when he describes the aircraft's response to the stick, the Youngman flaps, a system unique to Fairey aircraft (the company patented the device), give the Firefly a turning radius that belies its weight and size. Flap operation is hydraulic, and the devices can be deployed to the cruise position at 175 knots. Two hinge points in the flap—one on the leading edge and one at mid-chord—swing the flap back and down in such a way that it moves parallel to the wing chord line throughout its arc of travel. Once in position, airspeed can be increased to 250 knots. Even with the ingenious Youngman system, a Firefly was no match for such agile aerial cats as the Zero, and the British fighter relied on a diving one-chance-only pass at the target with all four cannons blazing. Any hit at all would stand a good chance of downing the comparatively lightly constructed Japanese types.

For landings, the leading edges of the flaps do not move downward but remain flush with the wing; only the mid-chord linkage arm moves out and down, deploying the flaps in the customary configuration.

The Heritage Firefly is one of very few operational Fireflys left in the world. For just plain keepin' on, this warplane has no peer. CF-BDH is symbolic of the wish of a devoted group of Canadians to render it the return favor of some tender loving care.

Sometimes a man and the plane he was meant to fly will remain strangers long into both their lives before they finally meet. Their meeting can be all the sweeter for that waiting. When it happens, this is what it can be like:

"Ol' Man West had two sons, and he taught them how to fly. Out of the cloudbursts of the war and into clear skies they flew, and still do, strapped into round-engine dusters, sitting up there bronzing in the sun.

"One day, J.K. swapped a run-out Stearman for a North American B-25. Swapped even. Now what kind of man would keep a B-25 for a pet? Brought it over to the local grass airport and it sat there hangar high. J.K. and his brother, Earl Junior, gave me a call: 'Hey, you wanna come ride the B-25?'

"It sits there all olive drab. The West boys are hunkering in the shade of a yellow-nosed nacelle plucking new grass. 'C'mon, boy.' I follow under the shade of the long, narrow belly to where it lets down its bib and climb up onto the flight deck and look down on the world. 'Sit in the right seat, boy.' Right in the tiger's mouth.

" 'You let me know when you see gas drippin' out of that one.'

" 'It's drippin'.'

"First a slow milling of the prop, then the blur and the shuddering cowl all wreathed in smoke.

" 'Don't see no flames either.'

" ' 'at's always a good sign.'

"We poise, tail out over the wire fence almost to the railroad tracks, with them little Cessnas cringing against their chains. J.K. does the run-up, twiddling mag switches from a '31 Packard dashboard, with its engine instruments all clustered in the middle like they were installed with a shotgun, and an artificial horizon big as a dinner plate. Right out of the Smithsonian.

" 'This thing working?'

" 'All them things is working.'

"My window slides shut easy, greasy, and (click) locks. Right then is when I decide to go on and trust those twenty-eight-year-old engines. If a man keeps a window track clean, you just know he takes care of the engines.

" 'I'll do this takeoff. The field is kind of short.'

"That's when it dawns on me that he's gonna let me . . . oh, lordy. Then he's pouring on the cobs and the seat back is crowding me. This twin island of rushing sound and all that tonnage is over the fence now, rattling kitchens below, and J.K. raises both paws off the wheel and smiles me my invitation. Just like that. I'm flying the Army Air Corps B-25 bomber, medium, twin-row Wright, 1,700 horsepower, tra la la.

"Take that, Army Air Corps. You were wrong about me, see? You washed me out in '43. I would have died for this, truly, but you gave me latrines to clean and garbage cans to dive, and the sandy, dusty stockade, and rides in the six-by truck with the chicken wire over the back and sloppy fatigues to wear while those other finks wore pinks and wings and little cookie-duster mustaches and fifty-mission caps. Oh, were you ever wrong about me! I laugh, thinking of all the tons of manuals they had to read to do this and here's ol' Colonel West giving it to me in the sweet essence—

" 'Hold 110 on approach . . . approach flaps coming now . . . gear coming down . . . I got a wheel . . .'

" 'I got a wheel.'

"I reel in some cable, and she turns sweetly onto final. A refinery slides by in the canted windshield. Another mood steals in: men died in planes just like this one, turning low over refineries. Metal opened, all jagged and shrieking wind. Turrets hammered and hot, spent .50-caliber brass rolled thick in new blood.

"I look down at the flight-deck floor, where cigarette butts roll thick in seed rice. The West boys smoke a lot and always have rice left over in their cuffs.

" 'Full flaps coming in now . . . hold 100.'

"You know all the pitch changes are moderate? Gear, flaps—all of it. J.K.'s heavy leg is pressed against the trim wheel, and I don't want to bother him so I just muscle it. No worse than a Cessna 182. Lining it up, I walk those tandem rudders—they're alive. Droop a wing for a little crosswind. She just stays wherever you put her; North American built stable airplanes. No wonder the Army hung onto its B-25s long after the other mediums had gone to aluminum pots. This great thing is four-by-four honest!

" 'Flies just like an airplane.'

" 'What'd you expect?'

"I flare a tad high, but she forgives me, settling in easier than a 310 would have. Then we try a few touch-and-goes, my teeth drying out because I can't quit grinning. Then it is brother Earl's turn, and I get up to move aft.

" 'Why you sweating so much, ace?'

" 'I was sitting in the sun.'

"The Brothers West flying together: the cockpit is just two Wests wide, and the harmony between them fairly sings. Earl has it easy—one hand—and I notice he pokes J.K.'s leg out of the way and flies the trim all the time. You watch, all the really good pilots do that. Earl makes a Stearman-size pattern, gets a squeaker.

" 'You wanna do another?'

" 'I wanna quit on that one.'

"The brothers laugh, light up and leave the hammer in on takeoff, gee-whizzing at the 30-foot-a-minute climb, and then go streaking off across rice fields, back to the grass airport.

" 'Hey, ain't that ol' Murph down there?'

" 'Yeah, that's his truck all right . . .'

"Ol' Murph is farming rice, riding high on a combine, sitting on almost every ticket the FAA ever issued and thousands of hours of dusting with the West boys. And you just know what's gonna happen to ol' Murph next, don't you?

"He never saw it coming nor heard it over the roar of the combine. It streaked between two harvesting machines umbrella high. Up, up into a duster turn, and down, tilting over the rice paddies. This is how it must have looked through Doolittle's windshield. Murph is out on the running board of the combine now, jumping up and down on his hat. It's Murph all right. He's a redhead. We go by again, pointing and waving out the side windows.

" 'Lookee ol' Murph! Haw haw, hee hee hee.'

"We wave out the window at about 200 knots. Going away, I think I see ol' Murph is trying to spell a four-letter word in the rice with his combine. We left a good swath harvested our own selves.

"The Wests, giants at play and at what they do for a living, were full of joy now. They left me off at the grass airport dancing with glee as the sweet harmony built up to a roar and the B-25 sucked up its gear, assumed its low, lethal silhouette, and bulleted for Angleton. What kind of men keep a B-25 for a pet? Some men putter it off at golf with little balls. Some men live grandly."

There are many interesting aircraft owners of classic airplanes, but one of the most unusual has to be Lex du Pont. If Alexis I. du Pont had been born a century earlier and hadn't been a scion of one of America's wealthier families, he'd have been a skilled shipwright, perhaps, or a maker of marvelous Conestoga wagons or the inventor of the cotton gin—or simply the most ingenious blacksmith in town. As it is, Lex du Pont is the owner and pilot of a Grumman FM-2 Wildcat—and the patron of a ramshackle collection of mechanical marvels called the Colonial Flying Corps Museum.

Du Pont is fascinated by things mechanical, and his hangar/museum/workshop on the New Garden Flying Field, Toughkenamon, Pennsylvania, is the incarnation of what you'd come up with if you prowled the barns and garages and airfields of forgotten America. Not "don't touch" display pieces or miracles of the restorer's art, but exactly what you'd get if you cleaned out this country's attic: a row of down-at-the-rims classic motorcycles culminating in a race-ready but rather tired Manx Norton; a well-used Morgan Three-Wheeler and a dusty HRG sports car; a beautiful yellow du Pont convertible that Lex still can't get started; rows and rows of small engines . . .

Turn a corner and there's a wingless Wildcat—a spare; turn another and there's a Tiger Moth being rebuilt. Look in a back room and you'll find a pair of Pittses under construction; walk outside and you'll have to duck under the tail booms of a decrepit P-38 sitting forlornly on flat tires, flanked by the cockpit/centersection of a Corsair and what might be the aft fuselage of a razorback Thunderbolt. There are crates and boxes and cabinets of what many would consider junk, but what men who honor the ingenuity of their predecessors know to be tiny milestones in man's mechanical quest.

Du Pont has the rough, raw-knuckled hands of a mechanic and the square, trimmed beard of an Amish farmer. He wears a wrench on his belt, tinted bifocals on his nose, and dresses in a manner quite unlike what you'd expect of the family that invented Better Living Through Chemistry. Naturally, he has a reputation as an eccentric. Actually, he is a kind of throwback to the days before planned obsolescence, when men took pride in the things they had devised, and the devices ran, or drove, or floated, or flew for as long as they were properly treated.

It is revealing that Lex still owns the Stinson L-5 in which he learned to fly fourteen years ago, as well as the Cessna 185 that he then bought as a traveling machine. He picked up the Wildcat in 1962, after having seen it several years before during one of his first cross-country solos as a student, and he has no intention of doing anything but continuing to fly it. Though he doubtless could if he wanted to, Lex has no interest in hopping from cockpit to cockpit in an ever-increasing spiral of conspicuous consumption. Each airplane means a great deal to him, and will maintain its fascination for as long as it's flyable. Not that he'd ever get bored: his hangar also holds a 450 Stearman, an SNJ, and a Ryan PT-22.

The museum and workshops are open to the public on a casual basis, if anyone's around to unlock the doors. Even if they're closed, New Garden is fast becoming a weekend Mecca for unusual, classic, and homebuilt airplanes.

The Grumman F4F Wildcat was a stubby grunt of a fighter, but it was built to last. It saved the day in the Pacific.

In June of 1942, after the Grumman Wildcat had become the mainstay fighter of the U.S. Navy and Marine Corps, Admiral Chester Nimitz, Commander-in-Chief, Pacific, damned it as "markedly inferior to the Japanese Zero fighter in speed, maneuverability and climb." Finally, it was shadowed into obscurity by such names as Hellcat, Corsair, Mustang, Spitfire, Lightning, Thunderbolt.

But had it not been for the Wildcat, and the dedicated people who built them and flew them so courageously, the war in the Pacific would have ended differently and perhaps tragically for the United States. The Wildcat was the staunch platform from which names such as Foss, Thach, Flatly,

O'Hare, Carl, Stanley, and Gayler became famous. The Wildcat was the root design that made possible both the Grumman TBF Avenger and the F6F Hellcat.

The Wildcat participated in many famous battles. The Nimitz summation went on to say:

> These characteristics [speed, maneuverability, and climb] must be improved, but not at the cost of overall superiority that in the Battle of Midway enabled our carrier fighter squadrons to shoot down about three Zero fighters for each of our own lost. However much of this superiority may exist in our splendid pilots, part at least rests in the armor, armament and leak-proof tanks of our planes.

Strategically, the Wildcat probably made one of its biggest combat contributions during the crucial defense of Guadalcanal (in August–November 1942). Later, teamed with the Grumman Avenger torpedo bomber, the plane functioned as part of a hunter-killer group to bring the U-boat war to a miserable end for the Germans.

The Grumman idea was to make it strong, make it work, and make it simple. If something didn't work, Grumman fixed it first and then argued the cost with the Navy later. Grumman also had noticeable empathy for pilots. Roy Grumman, who had flown for the Navy himself, handed down a mandatory design policy that said the cockpit would be the last component to fail during the total destruction of a Grumman aircraft.

The Grumman plant had become known in Navy circles as the Grumman Iron Works. Designer Bill Schwendler insisted that the design safety margin be more than the 5 percent required by the Navy. Sometimes the "Schwendler Factor" was two, other times it was three.

Though strong, the extremely narrow, roller-skate landing gear on the Wildcat caused endless ground loops. A pilot who says he never lost control of a Wildcat on the ground is probably either a liar or never flew one. This landing gear was manually operated (make it simple), and contributed significantly to the incomparable experience of getting the machine off the back on the ground. Some pilots needed to call upon every bit of flight training they had for the first hop. For others, that wasn't enough.

Let's start on the line. You've had your cockpit checkout. You're suspiciously examining a shotgun shell with which you've been told to start the engine. Gingerly, you place the shell into a breech so located that it might zap your kneecap, or worse, if the breech lock doesn't hold when you set off the fireworks. You prime the big 1800-series Pratt & Whitney, pump a little fuel pressure, crack the throttle, throw the starter switch. There's a hiss. The prop swings. There's a cough or two. Sputters run around the cowl. Suddenly, as the engine explodes into action, you're enveloped in the oil smoke that belches from the short exhaust stacks. Accompanied by vibration and noise, the smoke continues to blast into the cockpit. If you hold your breath for ten seconds, you won't asphyxiate and you'll eventually see the panel again.

While the engine warms, be sure the canopy is locked open, and remember to check that again before takeoff. You unlock the tailwheel and taxi. This reveals the brakes as marginal, at best. Use them too much and they'll fade permanently, and then you'll find out that to unfade the brakes, you need to rough up the linings with a stout metal file. Forget to open the cowl flaps? Fifteen turns of the crank will do it.

The otherwise routine checkoff list includes a couple of items of note. It says lock the tailwheel before takeoff. If you don't, you'll think you're in a swivel chair as soon as you get the throttle opened. You're asked to set in 2.5 degrees of right rudder. If this is your first flight, try 5 degrees. Then there is at least one informational item not on the checkoff list: tighten up the friction nut on the throttle quadrant enough so the throttle can't slip. Make it stubborn to move with conscious pressure. Failing this, you'll be in a frightening jam as you try to retract your landing gear in about sixty seconds from now, provided you actually get airborne. (If there's even a slight crosswind from the left, you probably won't get off the ground. Full right rudder, aileron to depress the right wing, and right brake all working together may not be enough to keep you going straight.)

Ease the tightened throttle forward to 46.5 inches and 2,600 rpm. Lead with right rudder and put a little back pressure on the stick to press that locked tailwheel hard down on the runway. You'll need its stabilizing effect. Even with all that rudder tab, you'll feel like you're holding full right rudder. Don't hesitate to add some right brake, if necessary. Now you're rolling. The rudder's more effective. You're going straight. Now neutralize the stick. You don't need to raise the tail. The fighter will three-point off at 70 to 75 knots.

You're off. The noise is unbelievable, so close the canopy. Ease back on the power. Best climb is 135. The noise is less now, but you'll remember to bring cotton next time. If you've never flown a fighter before, you'll be preoccupied with the speed. She's really moving out with the gear still down. She's sensitive. You'll notice you're holding left rudder now. Trim some of it out.

Now for the landing gear. You start by letting go of the throttle. You fly the plane with your left hand and prepare to crank the landing gear handle twenty-nine times. You switch the ratchet selector to up. Get a good grip on the handle and crank clockwise. The work is heavy, but once started, keep cranking until the gear is up and locked. If you let go with the gear partially retracted, the handle will spin wildly. Try to stop it, and you're sure to get a broken hand or wrist. If you fail to stop it, the bicycle chains and sprockets that operate the system are likely to foul, leaving you with inoperable gear guaranteed to cause trouble on landing. You're going to have enough of that with the gear properly down and locked.

Now you are flying with your left hand. With your right hand and arm, you're partway through the heavy task of cranking up the gear. You're breathing hard. You can't let go. You forgot to tighten the throttle enough. It slips back. Your power drops. You're becoming very busy.

Even without this avoidable difficulty, the gear-retraction procedure is about like trying to crank a car with one hand while holding a glass of champagne in the other. You could almost always tell a pilot was cranking his gear up before you could see the wheels move, by the sine-wave undulation of the airplane. An imposition on the pilot? Yes, but it did meet the Grumman strong-and-simple credo.

Landing the Wildcat was an event full of thrills. Once down, the machine was likely to dart off in any direction. The oleos would allow the wings to tilt, giving the pilot the feeling that the airplane was turning. The inexperienced would make a correction to stop the phantom turn. With the narrow landing gear, poor brakes, and a short moment from CG to rudder, loss of control was often quick and complete. The trick was to ignore the tilting wings, forget your sensations, and simply keep the nose glued on some landmark ahead. Once the characteristics of the Wildcat landing roll were understood (and remembered), pilots coped quite well. One form of amusement for naval air station personnel, however, was to watch a squadron return from a carrier after a long tour at sea. After landing only with the arresting gear, the best of pilots forgot. Several ground loops were certain entertainment.

Once airborne, the Wildcat was a pussycat. She'd come out of a ten-turn spin a quarter to half a turn. Both wings stalled at the same time. An inverted spin was a piece of cake. (Inverted spins were part of the Navy training syllabus in those days.) The Wildcat could be managed in level flight at 50 knots with gear and split flaps down, making 10-degree turns. This wasn't for the new boy, but it was part of operational training in some squadrons.

The differences in design concepts between the Zero and the Wildcat became visible at Guadalcanal. Many historians believe this battle was pivotal; that had the United States lost there, the war would have certainly had a different, probably tragic, outcome for us. Had we not had the Wildcats, our defeat there would have been assured. While the Avengers and the Douglas Dauntless dive bombers did the killing damage to the attacking Japanese naval and amphibious forces, the Wildcats made their action possible.

The Japanese, based at Rabaul, were attempting to eliminate our Henderson Field at Guadalcanal with twin-engine Betty bombers escorted by Zeros. Control of the island would have provided the Japanese with capability to strike at the Allied supply line to Australia, provide air cover for operations against the New Hebrides, and interfere seriously with American landings within the Solomon Islands. Much was at stake.

The Mitsubishi Bettys were perhaps the finest twin-engine medium bombers extant, and were nearly as fast at cruising altitude as was the F4F at maximum speed. The Betty had more than adequate range. The Zeros were superbly designed to be superior in speed, climb, and maneuverability to the Wildcat. With belly tanks attached, the Zeros could complete the 950-nautical-mile round trip with the bombers, but overall combat performance was reduced slightly by the tanks, which could not be dropped if the planes were to return to Rabaul. Neither Japanese plane had armor or self-sealing fuel tanks, but even with these handicaps, Zeros were lethal opponents and maintained the upper hand in many situations.

Our F4F pilots had learned that the overhead pass was most effective against bombers. The attacking fighter, flying in the opposite direction, would invert and dive. This is a particularly difficult maneuver to do with precision. Major J. N. Renner, USMC, in a 1943 interview, discussed dogfighting tactics with the F4F against the Zero:

> We used tactics developed by Foss, Bauer and Smith. In order to knock Zeros down, the Grummans stuck together. Each pilot paid less attention to the man on his tail than to the Zero on somebody else's tail. Once a dogfight started, we all revolved around the same area. If a Zero dived out from the dogfight, our instructions were not to follow him but to swing back to the middle of the merry-go-round. In swinging back, you look for a Zero on some other Grumman's tail. A Zero can't take two seconds fire from a Grumman. A Grumman can sometimes take as high as fifteen minutes' fire from a Zero. It's damn hard to instill in a pilot the idea that even though there's somebody on his tail, he's got to work on the guy that's on another's tail. That's exactly what we did, and it worked out successfully.

However, when a Zero was on a Grumman, and there was no other Grumman to take care of the Zero, the Grumman pilot had one more ace in the hole. He could dive with full throttle and have an excellent chance of getting away, thanks to the famous Schwendler Factor.

The Wildcat delivered a kill ratio of 6.9 to 1. There is no breakdown as to type of kills—fighters or bombers—but the conclusion is inescapable that aside from the design concepts the Wildcat pioneered, the final score against the Zero has to be on the side of the Grumman Iron Works.

There are very few Wildcats left today. Only seven are known to be still flying, according to Grumman historian Andrew Hubbard. One beautiful specimen is that owned by the Colonial Flying Corps Museum and is available for the public to see, admission free.

In Pennsylvania, a Wildcat still flies. In other skies, such as over California, old Japanese warbirds, including some Zeros, are taken up by fliers zealous to preserve man's aeronautical heritage. The battles are over, but the warbirds' significance to aviation and their beauty remain. They represent a twilight zone in sport flying, a vague boundary area where flying unusual aircraft for sheer fun blends into a communing with the past, as these pilots man cockpits in which the hopes of nations once rode.

CONCLUSION: *Something Well Worth Having*

PEOPLE often jokingly say that if God had meant people to fly, he would have given them wings. They miss the point. He gave us minds and imagination to fly higher than any bird.

To fly over open country, to fly just for the sake of flying, is to know freedom. Not just to *feel* free, which can be mere delusion, but to *know* it, to be aware that you are totally free. In flight, the world is open to you. Light is a message, a dialogue, in which the sun and clouds and the radiance of the land are all participants; at night, it is radiated in pinpoints of brilliance that mark autos, towns, isolated houses, and huge cities. Even in cloud, flight means the freedom from or the mastery of that which we normally fear, for flight in cloud can mean the mastery of intelligence over mystery.

Below the pilot hills swell upward in green splendor; highways dart hither and yon, doubling upon themselves at times, as if to mark points of introspection; gashes, craters, cliffs, rivers, bays, volcanoes, cities punctuate the land. All these the pilot sees from above. He can see where all is well—where all has been left well or made well—and where mistakes have been made. The joys well outnumber the griefs.

The best joy is flight itself: to know you are *up there*, seeing from where you see, feeling the coolness of new breezes, making for yourself the choices of involvement or detachment, and knowing, above all, that for the moment you are a completely separate entity.

To follow the line of a road as it winds among trees, to follow one's shadow along the ground, to circle above uncaring cattle, to float among mountains, to flit mere feet above the ground, to blast one's way through a gaggle of high-powered machines, to feel the power of flight against one's feet and in one's hands, to fly—there is, quite simply, no other way of life like it. Here, the significant words are not "feeling" or "sensation," for those suggest things quickly sensed and gone. No. Once savored, flight becomes an unbreakable habit, a state of being to be assumed whenever possible. Even as a passenger, one can develop this kind of passion, but it is only as a pilot, as a wielder of the controls, where freedom is complete, that one can be totally engulfed by the pilot's love of his craft.

The sense of freedom to move in space is rather like the freedom one has in swimming underwater, but no water was ever so clear, nor seascape so vast, as the air and the lands beneath. People who can ride in an airplane and feel no sense, no hint of the exultation of wonderment and awe, are the despair of pilots, who feel that they ought to be able to point with a gesture to the surrounding world and cast over their passengers a spell of wide-eyed admiration. It doesn't always work, but it ought to. There is really nothing like flying in a small airplane, especially one with big windows, on a stormy summer afternoon with the towering clouds spouting all around, the slanting rainfalls here and there, the green ground mottled with light and shadow, the visible layers of air like stacked sheets of glass in different shades of green and blue. There is nothing like the movement of it: the deliberate grace of a wingover turn, the quiet swoop of a turning slip to a landing, or the upward tug of the wings and the sudden smoothness as the wheels leave the runway, the wings take over from them, and the bond to the ground is broken.

Language does not have words to describe the experiences of flight. It is as difficult now—for all the millions of hours flown by millions of people—to describe flight as it was at the beginning. If you have not done it yourself, you cannot imagine it. But to be a passenger merely, taking in the feeling and the view, is only part of it. The other part is the pleasure of operating an airplane, of being the controller of the arc and swooping, of having the stick in your hands and with small pressures on it dipping a wing, pulling up, wheeling over as the blazing sun swings across the windshield, and then gently pulling back as the nose turns toward the earth and the rush of the wind grows shriller. Or swerving between the boiling walls of clouds close enough to touch them, or resting in silence atop an invisible column of air, seeming to turn about one wing tip. Or just going, on those days when all the vibrations seem to fall into velvety step, when the air is cold and like still water and you can fly at a thousand feet, sliding over the lakes and roads and towns, glimpsing instants in a thousand early morning lives—just flying for the sheer fun of it.

Flying is not cheap; fine things usually aren't. It will never be an activity available to huge numbers of people, as skiing or boating are, both because of its cost (though passionate devotees here, as elsewhere, find ways around costs) and because there is not room in the air for limitless numbers of airplanes. But of all the sports and diversions man has contrived for himself, it is surely the most vast in its scope and the most moving. No king, "lord of all he surveys," or explorer looking with wild surmise upon some newfound ocean, sees what a pilot sees, or feels what he may feel, if he can only keep his sense of wonder and beauty alive.

Down on the ground, we are like the blind men with their fragmentary ideas of the elephant. From a mountaintop we may see more, but from an airplane we see enough to know what this elephantine earth truly is, to know its complexion and expressions, and then on top of this, to dance in such a place, above that face, to do our gymnastics and our gambols between God and the ground—that is the closest this life will bring us to sporting with angels.

Flying as a sport is hard to master, costly, often frustrating. It requires a good pilot and a good airplane, and it is often difficult to bring the two together. It is a use of fuel for the sake of pleasure rather than business and will come under fire from here and there as the years of fossil fuels grow fewer; it may be ecologically objectionable in some contexts, and some of the habits of the past will have to be changed for the sake of people's peace and quiet. Some sorts of sport flying may be less defensible than others when the battle lines are drawn, and no doubt a better case can be made for balloons and gliders than for surplus fighters and bombers. There will always be a place for homebuilts, as long as there are engines and ideas to hang them on. Extinction is far off, and while there is the possibility of flying for fun, it is worth exploiting and fighting for. When it is no longer possible—a time that may be forty or fifty years, or more, away—those who will have done it will have the memories of kings. They will have trod an Atlantis that is no more to be found; their dreams will be richer than those of others, and they will have a larger sense of the possibilities of this shriveling world.

APPENDIX: *Pilot Licensing*

BASIC REQUIREMENTS

MEDICAL CERTIFICATES

Before you can learn how to fly, one of the first requirements you will have to fulfill is to obtain a third-class medical certificate. This is done by passing a physical examination given by an FAA-certified doctor. It will also serve as your student pilot license. When your instructor endorses it, it will become your license to solo. If your medical certificate expires, you may not exercise the privileges of being a pilot.

The second-class medical certificate is required of commercial pilots, and the first-class, of airline-transport-rated pilots. A brief comparison of the physical requirements follows, so that you may see the differences from class to class. You may obtain a medical certificate for a higher rating than you hold, and many pilots do so as a means of maintaining and demonstrating good general health.

THIRD CLASS
valid 24 calendar months after month of issue.
eyes correctable to 20/30 in each eye; red, green, white color discrimination.
ears, nose, throat, equilibrium and nervous system within normal limits.
cardiovascular no history of heart disease.
general health good.
rejection diabetes requiring drug for control, alcoholism, epilepsy, drug addiction and psychotic behavior.

SECOND CLASS
valid 12 calendar months after month of issue.

eyes 20/100 or better, correctable to 20/20 in each eye; red, green, white color discrimination, normal field of vision.
ears, nose, throat, equilibrium and nervous system within normal limits.
cardiovascular no history of heart disease.
general health good.
rejection diabetes requiring drug for control, alcoholism, epilepsy, drug addiction and psychotic behavior.

FIRST CLASS
valid 6 calendar months after month of issue.
eyes 20/100 or better, correctable to 20/20 in each eye; no color blindness, normal field of vision.
ears, nose, throat, equilibrium and nervous system within normal limits.
cardiovascular no history of heart disease; annual EKG after age 35.
general health good.
rejection diabetes requiring drug for control, alcoholism, epilepsy, drug addiction and psychotic behavior.

WAIVERS AND EXEMPTIONS

For persons who may not be able, for one reason or another, to pass their medical examinations, the FAA has special procedures.

The most common area that is waived in FAA medicals is that of visual defects. There are several others where either a waiver or an exemption may obtain. The loss of a limb, for example, may be exempted through a *medical flight test*—during which a pilot must prove competence consistent with air safety.

233

Even certain apparently impossible cases, such as diabetes or coronary disease, can be dealt with by the granting of special time-limited medical certificates. Where a diabetic has satisfactorily achieved a stabilized regime by diet, for example, the FAA might grant a certificate good for six months. If you are in doubt, a talk with your regional flight surgeon's office at the FAA could be helpful. Further details may be found in FAR 67.19.

PRIVATE CERTIFICATE

STUDENT
You must be at least 16 years old.
You must have:
- a command of the English language
- a third-class medical certificate
- a Federal Communications Commission radio-operator's permit.

SOLO
Your medical certificate must be signed by a certified flight instructor for the type of airplane you are flying.

PRIVATE
You must be at least 17 years old when you take the FAA flight check, and your medical certificate must be current at that time.

Your instructor must be satisfied that you understand the necessary operating rules and limitations in the *Federal Aviation Regulations.*

You must have passed the FAA private pilot written examination with a score of 70 or better. You must have an understanding of and be able to answer questions about:
- the FARs applicable to the private pilot
- the National Transportation Safety Board's regulations

- the *Airman's Information Manual*
- basic meteorology

for the oral exam given at the time of the flight check.

You must be proficient in preflight, starting and running up the engine, takeoffs and landings, traffic-pattern procedures, basic flight control, straight-and-level flight, climbing and gliding turns, stalls and recoveries and various emergency procedures.

You must have had a minimum of 40 hours of flight time, broken down into:
- 20 hours of dual instruction signed by a certified flight instructor, of which:
  - three hours are cross-country (a trip with a landing at least 25 miles from the home base)
  - three hours are night flying with a minimum of 10 takeoffs and landings
  - three hours are dual review, signed by your CFI, before the flight check;
- 20 hours of solo flight, of which:
  - 10 are cross-country trips with landings at least 50 miles from the home base, and one trip with three landings, each 100 miles apart
  - and in which three takeoffs and landings are made at a controlled field.

The flight check will include:
- the maneuvers required for solo plus advanced stalling maneuvers, turns about a point and special landings and takeoffs
- navigation by charts, compass and radio aids
- flight with sole reference to instruments.

INSTRUMENT RATING

You must have:
- a current private certificate with the

appropriate aircraft rating and corresponding medical certificate
- FCC radio-operator's permit.

You must have passed the FAA instrument rating written examination with a score of 70 or better. You must have an understanding of and be able to answer questions on:
- the FARs applicable to the instrument pilot
- the *Airman's Information Manual*
- the instrument air-traffic system
- dead reckoning applicable to IFR operations
- VOR, ADF and ILS systems
- approach plates and charts
- applicable meteorology

for the oral exam given at the time of the flight check.

You must have had a minimum of 200 logged hours, broken down into:
- 100 hours of pilot-in-command time
- 50 hours of cross-country in the type of airplane for which the rating is being sought
- 40 hours of instrument time (up to 20 hours may be in a simulator)
- 15 hours of dual instrument instruction from a CIFI
- one cross-country flight of at least 250 miles under instrument conditions.

The flight check will include:
- flight with sole reference to instruments
- navigation
- work with air-traffic control
- instrument approaches
- emergency procedures.

MULTI-ENGINE RATING

You must be at least 17 years old.

You must have:
- made at least five takeoffs and landings either solo or as pilot-in-command with a pilot rated to carry passengers in that aircraft
- passed an appropriate flight test.

Although it is not specified in the FARs, most examiners like to see a minimum of 10 hours' flight time in type logged before the check ride. The actual exam consists of:
- a question and answer session in which you will be expected to answer questions regarding airplane registration, airworthiness and equipment documents, airplane logbooks and airworthiness reports, airplane performance parameters, loading calculations—including fuel, oil and baggage capacities, preflight check and use of radio for voice communication
- basic piloting techniques including preflight operations, taxiing, normal and crosswind takeoffs and landings, steep turns, stalls and partial stalls, short-field takeoffs and landings and emergency go-arounds. If instrument rated, you will have to demonstrate your ability to fly by instruments in a multi-engine airplane
- multi-engine emergency procedures including (a) maneuvering with one engine out (feathered if possible); (b) engine-out minimum-control-speed demonstration; (c) use of engine-out best-rate-of-climb speed (d) effect on engine-out performance of failing to feather, extension of gear and flaps, and combinations of them; and (e) approach and landing with an engine set for zero thrust, or the drag of a feathered propeller
- showing that you know how all the aircraft's emergency systems work, and when to use them.

COMMERCIAL CERTIFICATE

You must be 18 years old at the time of the flight check.

You must have:
- a second-class medical certificate
- an instrument rating, or a restriction prohibiting the carrying of passengers at night or for hire on a cross-country flight of more than 50 miles
- an FCC radio-operator's permit.

You must have passed the FAA commercial pilot written examination with a score of 70 or better.

You must have an understanding of and be able to answer questions about:
- the FARs applicable to the commercial pilot
- the *Airman's Information Manual*
- basic aerodynamics and principles of flight
- the operation of a complex airplane (one with retractable gear and a controllable-pitch propeller)
- weight-and-balance computations
- applicable meteorology

for the oral examination given at the time of the flight check.

You must have a minimum of 250 hours of logged flight time, broken down into:
- up to 50 hours in a simulator
- 50 hours of dual instruction including:
  - 10 hours in a complex airplane
  - 10 hours instrument training
  - 10 hours review preparing for the flight check;
- 100 hours pilot-in-command time, including:
  - 50 hours of cross-country, including a flight with landings at three points, each 200 miles apart

- five hours of night flying, including at least 10 takeoffs and landings.

The flight check will include:
- basic and complex maneuvers
- complex-airplane operation
- emergency procedures.

CERTIFIED FLIGHT INSTRUCTOR

You must be at least 18 years old.

You must have:
- a commercial certificate with an instrument rating
- an FCC radio-operator's permit
- a second-class medical certificate.

You must pass the FAA certified flight instructor written examination with a score of 70 or better.

You must have an understanding of and be able to answer questions about:
- the learning process
- elements of teaching
- evaluation of student performance
- lesson planning
- instruction techniques
- analysis and correction of common student errors

for the oral examination given at the time of the flight check.

The flight check will include:
- performance and analysis of the standard flight training procedures and maneuvers appropriate to the rating sought.

AIR TRANSPORT RATING

You must have:
- full command of the English language

without accent or impediment that might interfere with radio communication

- a first-class medical certificate without waivers
- a commercial license without limitations or military experience that can qualify you under FAR 61.31 for a commercial pilot certificate.

You must have passed the FAA written exam, which will include questions about:

- FARs, Parts 61, 121, 65, 91, 21, 15
- fundamentals of air navigation, including the use of formulas, instruments and other navigational aids, necessary to instrument navigation
- the overall weather system, including systems presentation and nomenclature; elementary meteorology and factors that affect aeronautical activities
- weight-and-balance procedures.

You must have logged a minimum of 1,500 hours total time, broken down into:

- 250 hours as pilot-in-command of which at least 100 hours are cross-country and 25 hours night flying
- at least 500 hours cross-country and 100 hours night and 75 hours instruments, of which 25 hours may be simulator time.

The flight check will include:

- all maneuvers applicable to the type of aircraft in which the applicant is tested, and consistent with the ratings held.

GLIDER CATEGORY

STUDENT

You must be at least 14 years old and have signed a statement as to your good general health.

SOLO

PRIVATE

You must be at least 16 years old when the flight check is taken.

You must have passed the FAA glider private pilot written examination with a score of 70 or better.

You must have an understanding of and be able to answer questions on:

- the FARs pertinent to the private glider pilot
- the National Transportation Safety Board's regulations
- basic meteorology

for the oral exam at the time of the flight check.

You must be proficient in takeoffs and landings, glides and gliding turns and recoveries from stalls.

You must have had a minimum of:

- 70 solo flights, of which 20 include 360-degree turns
- a minimum of seven hours of solo flight (at least 35 flights from a ground tow or 20 flights from an air tow)

or

- 40 hours of total time in gliders and single-engine land airplanes, including at least 10 flights in a glider with 360-degree turns
- the basic maneuvers required for solo
- navigation by charts and compass
- towing procedures
- precision maneuvers.

LIGHTER-THAN-AIR CATEGORY

STUDENT

You must be at least 16 years old (14 for free balloons).

You must have:
- a third-class medical certificate (in the case of a free-balloon student, a signed statement of general good health is all that is required)
- an FCC radio-operator's permit.

Your instructor must be sure that you have an understanding of the *Federal Aviation Regulations* applicable to lighter-than-air flight.

You must have passed the FAA lighter-than-air private pilot written examination with a score of 70 or better.

You must have an understanding of and be able to answer questions about:
- the FARs applicable to lighter-than-air pilots
- the effects of superheating and positive and negative lift
- basic meteorology

for the oral exam given at the time of the flight check.

You must be proficient in preflight checks, use of hot-air sources (if applicable), liftoffs and climbs, descents and landings, emergency procedures and, in the case of airships, rigging, ballasting, controlling pressure and superheating as well as landings with positive and negative static balance.

You must have had a minimum of 50 hours of flight time for an airship rating, broken down into a minimum of 25 hours in airships, including five hours of solo flight.

You must have had a minimum of 10 hours of flight time for a free-balloon rating, broken down into:
- a minimum of six flights under the supervision of a commercial free-balloon pilot
- two flights, each of one hour's length if gas balloon, 30 minutes if hot air
- one ascent to 5,000 feet above ground level if gas balloon, 3,000 feet if hot air balloon is used
- six flights in a free balloon under supervision of a commercial free-balloon pilot, including at least one solo flight.

The flight check will include:
- ground handling
- takeoffs and landings with static lift
- straight-and-level flight, climbs, turns and descents
- precision maneuvering
- navigation
- emergency procedures.

The flight check for free balloons will include:
- rigging and mooring
- operation of burner
- ascents and descents
- landings
- emergency procedures, including (simulated) use of ripcord.

Photo Credits

Grateful acknowledgment is made for pictures used from the following sources:

Aero-Graphics, p. 1
Norbert Aubuchon, p. 222
James Collison, pp. 180, 182, 183
Flying Magazine Archives, title page, pp. 2,
    5, 45, 55, 57, 59, 65, 69, 72, 73, 106, 107,
    114, 123, 162, 167, 186
Paul Garrison, pp. 147, 148, 149, 150, 153
Peter Garrison, pp. 174, 177, 178
James Gilbert, pp. 25, 28, 29, 33, 34, 74, 76,
    78 (bottom), 80, 83, 84, 87, 88, 89, 95, 118,
    120, 124, 169, 189, 197
Hans Groenhoff, p. 35
E. Hansen, p. 38 (top)
Imperial War Museum, p. 66
Jim Larsen, p. 62

George C. Larson, p. 214
Nyle Leatham, pp. 7, 10, 31, 38 (bottom)
Peter Lert, p. 130
Jim Lizzio, pp. 50, 51, 53
Ed Mack Miller, p. 97
Lester W. Nelson, Jr., pp. 198, 199, 201
Jennifer Richardson, pp. 117, 131
Norbert Slepyan, pp. 100, 116, 126
Gene Thomas, pp. 12, 14, 16, 18, 22
Frank A. Tinker, p. 20
Archie Trammell, pp. 75, 77, 78 (top), 82, 92
Universal Studios, pp. 40, 43
Richard B. Weeghman, pp. 104, 111
Ann Welch, p. 142
Stephan Wilkinson, pp. 27, 192, 193, 204

Acknowledgment is also given for the photographs in the color section between
pages 118 and 119:

Balloon, Carl Roodman
Restoration, *Flying* Magazine Archives
B-25, Russell Munson
Grumman J2F-2, *Flying* Magazine Archives
Unlimiteds, *Flying* Magazine Archives
Ballooning groundwork, Carl Roodman

Waco Meteors, Budd Davisson
Fairey Firefly, George C. Larson
The Snowbirds, George Hall
Waco UPF-7, Stephan Wilkinson
Sailplane, Howell Conant

Index

Aerobatics, 6–36; aircraft suited for, 9, 26–36; anxiety and, 9–11; basic maneuvers in, 11–19; definition of, 6; styles of flying, 19–26

Aeronca Champion airplane, 30

Aileron roll, 15

Aircraft Cylinder, Inc., 94

Air racing, 64–65, 67–85; appeal of, 79–85; first races, 63–64, 67; popularity of, in 1930s, 68–71; requirements for, 75–79; revival of, 71–75

Akrostar airplane, 28

Alliance Argo airplane, 198

Apache airplane, 47

Armstrong, Neil, 160

AS-W12 sailplane, 128

AS-W15 sailplane, 132

AS-W17 sailplane, 132, 137, 139, 140

AT-6 airplane, 45, 73, 77, 78, 98, 193

Avro 540 airplane, 200

Ax, Goran, 134, 140

AX-6 balloon, 152, 155

B-25 bomber, 47, 217, 218, 219, 220

B-25 Mitchell airplane, 211

Ballooning, 146–60; sensation of, 146–51; technique of, 151, 154–60

Barone, George, 203, 204, 205, 207, 208

Barrel roll, 15

Batterson, Ann, 53

Bearcat airplanes, 44, 46, 74, 76, 78, 83, 211. *See also* Conquest I

Bell Aircraft Company, 71

Bellanca Champion Decathlon airplane, 30–33

Bellanca Citabria (aerobatic training plane), 30, 31, 32

Bell P-39 Airacobra airplane, 211

Bell P-63 Kingcobra airplane, 211

Beltz, Tom, 141, 144

Bendix Trophy Race, 75, 76

Betty bomber, 226–27

BE-2C observation plane, 202

Bezak, Ladislav, 34

Bikle, Paul F., 128, 129

Blériot, Louis, 194

Blériot airplane, 200

Boeing F4B1 airplane, 44

Boeing P-12 airplane, 189

Boeing P-26 airplane, 189

Bogart, Humphrey, 37

Boland, Bruce, 86

Bonzo airplane, 71

Boston Sky Club, 111

Bradley, Kennis, 215

Bradney (pilot), 138

Building airplanes, 161–84; homebuilt planes, 166–71; *Melmoth* project, 172–84

Canadian Warplanes Heritage, Inc., 213

Cartry, Jean Pierre, 140

Cassidy, Mel, 89

Catch-22 (motion picture), 39–42

Cat's Cradle, 129–30

Century-Series jet fighter, 44

Cessna airplanes, 29, 83, 170, 219, 221

Chance-Vought F4U Corsair airplane, 211

Chanute, Octave, 109

Churchill, Winston, 193

Citabria. *See* Bellanca Citabria

Cleland, Cook, 96

Cobham, Alan, 194

Cobra airplane, 136

Cochran, Jacqueline, 68

Colonial Flying Corps Museum, 220, 228

Competitive soaring, 124–45; Cat's Cradle, 129–30; first world meet, 127; kinds of, 125–27; "off-field" landings, 129; procedure for, 128–29; speed criteria, 120; standard and open-class, 132–33; standards of achievement in, 127–28; techniques and stratagems, 131–32; world championship contests, 133–45; world distance record, 128

Conquest I airplane, 78, 86–98; crew, 86–87; design modifications, 87–91; electrical system, 90; engine, 91, 94; exhaust blast, 94–95; litigation over, 98; power and speed of, 92, 95, 97, 98; record run (1969), 96

Convair airplane, 92

Cooper, Gary, 37

Corsair P-38 airplane, 74

Corsair P-39 airplane, 74

Cote, Ray, 80

Cousins, Dr. Phil, 98

Cuban eight maneuver, 16

Curtiss, Glenn, 67

Curtiss Aircraft Company, 71

Curtiss P-40 airplane, 45, 211

Curtiss pusher, 69

DC-6 airplane, 92

Decathlon airplane, 30–32

Delafield, John, 140

Doolittle, Jimmie, 68

Douglas AD-1 Skyraider airplane, 91

Douglas B-26 airplane, 74, 76, 211

Downey, Bob, 83

Drop zone (DZ), 51, 55

Du Pont, Alexis I., 220–21

Edwards Air Force Base, 93

Eipper, Dick, 109

El Toro Marine Corps Air Station, 47

F6F Hellcat airplane, 87, 223

F8F Bearcat airplane, 211

F8F-1 Bearcat airplane, 87, 89

F8F-2 Bearcat airplane, 86, 87

Fairchild airplanes, 198

Faust, Joe, 110

Federal Aviation Administration (FAA), 29, 104, 110, 123, 154, 166, 171, 181

Fédération Aéronautique Internationale (FAI), 127, 128, 138, 140, 141

Fighter Aircraft Museum, 96

Fighter Imports, 211

Fighter planes. *See* Warplanes

Firefly airplane, 213–17

Fitchett, Bernard, 142

Flaherty, Bob, 86

Fleet airplane, 198

Flight of the Phoenix, The (motion picture), 42

Flying (magazine), 176

FM-2 Wildcat airplane, 220–28

Focke-Wulf 190 airplane, 211, 212

Fokker D.VII airplane, 196, 200

Formula One airplanes, 64, 65, 71, 73, 79, 80, 81, 83, 84, 92

Fornof, Bill, 93, 94

Fox Airfield, 49

Free fall. *See* Skydiving

Gaffaney, Mary, 28

Galloway, Bev, 159, 160

Garrison, Peter, 172–84

General Aviation District Office, 154

G-forces, 12–14, 15, 25–26, 64

Glasflugel Standard Libelle sailplane, 132

Gliders. *See* Sailplanes

Gliding Federation of Australia, 143

Goodhart, Nick, 136

Goodyear races (Cleveland, 1949), 72, 73

Gordon, Walter, 142

Grant, Cary, 37

Granville Gee Bees, 70

Great Waldo Pepper, The (motion picture), 40, 43

Greenamyer, Darryl, 74, 78, 86–98
Greene, Ben, 134, 135, 137, 141
Grosse, Hans-Werner, 128, 140, 144
Grumman Aircraft Company, 39, 47, 71, 211, 220–28
Guadalcanal, defense of (1942), 223
Gypsy Moth airplane, 200

Haemmerle, Andreus, 140
Hammerhead maneuver, 17–19, 24, 32
Hang gliding, 103–12; clubs and organizations, 110–11; cost of equipment, 104; FAA and, 110; requirements for, 104–5; Rogallo "kite," 108–10; ski-slope, 105–6; types of, 103
Harrah's Club (Reno), 75
Havilland, Captain Geoffrey de, 191–95
Hawker Sea Fury airplane, 74
Hawker Siddeley Aircraft Company, 196
Herendeen, Bob, 47
Hillard, Charlie, 26–27, 28
Holden, William, 37
Holighaus, Klaus, 139–40
Hollywood-Burbank Airport, 75
Homemade airplanes, 166–71; cost of, 168; engines for, 168–70; FAA requirements for, 166, 171; Melmoth project, 172–84; test flight, 170–71; types of, 168
Hoover, Bob, 65, 98
Howard, Ben, 68, 76, 189
Hubbard, Andrew, 228

Icarus II biplane, 109
Immelmann turn, 16
Innes (pilot), 138
Inverted flight maneuvers, 24–26

Jenny airplane, 200
Jensen, Volmer, 109
Johnson, Richard, 125–27, 134, 135, 140
Jumping. See Skydiving

Kepka, Franciszek, 134, 142
Kerchenfaut, Bill, 86
Kestrel 17 sailplane, 135
Kestrel 19 sailplane, 132, 136
Kiceniuk, Taras, 109
Kilbourne, Dave, 109
King, Richard, 195–202
Kinner airplane, 198
Korean War, 211, 213
Krumme, Karl, 176
Krutch, Joseph Wood, 37

Lacy, Clay, 75, 81
Lambie, Jack, 111
Law, Pete, 86
L/D (lift-to-drag ratio), 115–16
Le Blond airplane, 198
Lee, Brian, 144
Lilienthal, Otto, 103, 109
Lockheed P-38 Lightning airplane, 211
Lomcovak, 22–24, 32, 34
Loop maneuvers, 8, 9, 12–14
Los Angeles Air Races, 93
Low and Slow (ed. Faust), 110
LS-2 sailplane, 143
Lyford, Chuck, 97

Macchi-Castoldi seaplane, 68
Mahler, Ed, 8
Maneuvers, types of, 11–19
Mantz, Paul, 42
March Air Force Base, 152
McMain, Cecil, 86
Melmoth, 172–84; christened, 178–79; construction of, 172–76; cost and expenses, 175–76; test flights, 178–84
Mercier, Michel, 142
Messerschmitt 109 airplane, 211
Mig-17 jet, 34
Miles Master airplane, 193
Miller, Richard, 109

Mister Mulligan (racer), 76, 189
Moffat, George, 134, 135, 137, 139, 140, 142, 144
Mojave 1,000 Race, 73, 75, 81, 98
Montgomery, John, 109
Morland, Howard, 179
Murphy's War (motion picture), 44
Mustang airplane, 74, 76–78, 83, 210, 212

National Advisory Committee for Aeronautics (NACA), 71
National Aeronautic Association, 128
New Garden Flying Field, 220
Nietlispach (pilot), 135, 136
Nieuport 28 airplane, 200
Nimbus II sailplane, 132, 139, 140
Nimitz, Admiral Chester, 222, 223
North American Aircraft Company, 71

"Off-field" landings, 129
Old airplanes, nostalgia for, 185–232
Orange County Airport, 44
O'Toole, Peter, 44
Otto Lilienthal Soaring Meet, 111
OX5 airplane, 198

P-38 airplane, 46
P-40 airplane, 44–45
P-51 Mustang airplane, 44–45, 47, 94, 211
P-51H Mustang airplane, 91
Palen, Cole, 196, 197
Palen airplane, 200
Parachute Club, 54
Parachuting. *See* Skydiving
Pattersson (pilot), 138
Penaud (pilot), 142
Perris Trolley Museum, 152
Petroczy (pilot), 136
Piccard, Don, 152–59
Piccard family, 152–53

Pik-20 sailplane, 143, 144
Piper Cub airplane, 195, 198
Pitch change, rate of, 9
Pitts, Paw (Curtis), 28–29
Pitts Special biplane, 26–30, 32, 170
Poberezny, Tom, 26–27
Poe, Ray, 86
Professional Race Pilot's Association, 98
Puss Moth airplane, 200

R-1 Gee Bee airplane, 70
R-2 Gee Bee airplane, 70
Racing. *See* Air racing
Raft, George, 37
Ragot, François, 136, 139, 140
Rate information, 9
Reading Air Show, 205
Red Devils, 26–27
Reichmann, Helmut, 134, 135, 136, 137, 142
Renner, Ingo, 142
Renner, Major J. N., 227
Reno Unlimited Race, 86
Republic P-47 Thunderbolt airplane, 211
Rheims Meeting of 1909, 67
Rhinebeck Aerodrome, 195
Robertson, Cliff, 193
Robinson, Edward G., 37
Rogallo, Francis M., 108
Rogallo flex wing, 105, 108–10
Rollasons Company, 193
Rolling turn maneuver, 24
Roll maneuver, 14–17
Rudensky (pilot), 135
Ryan PT-22 airplane, 221

S-2 airplane, 29
Sailplanes, 113–45
SB-10 sailplane, 133
Schneider Trophy, 67–68
Scholl, Art, 3, 21, 47

Schweizer 1-23E sailplane, 128
Schweizer 1-26 sailplane, 132
Schweizer 2-32 sailplane, 124
Schwendler, Bill, 223
Scoville, Randy, 86
Seabees, 39
Showmanship, 37–48; in the movies, 37, 39–44, 48
Sky Ranch Airport, 88
Skydiving, 49–60, 151; drop zone (DZ), 51, 55; exit procedure, 49–52; hitting the ground, 58–60; lore, 55–58
Slow roll maneuver, 15–16
Smith, A. J., 134, 135, 138
Smith Miniplane, 170
Snap roll maneuver, 16–17, 21, 23, 32
Snipe airplane, 200
SNJ airplane, 221
Soaring, 113–23; air pollutants and, 117, 121; competitive, 125–45; essence of, 113–14; lift-to-drag ratio, 115–16, 117; lore of, 122–24; panoramic observations, 120–21; sound and noise in, 118–20; temperature differences, 120
Soaring Society of America, 110, 144
Sonnichsen, Deke, 152, 159, 160
Sopwith airplane, 195–202
Soucy, Gene, 26–27
Southern California Hang Glider Association, 110–11
Spad airplane, 200
Speed, 8, 61–98; in competitive soaring, 130; racing, 67–85; records, 86–98
Spin maneuver, 11
Spitfire airplane, 193, 211, 212
Sport Biplanes, 73, 78–79, 83
Standard Cirrus sailplane, 132, 134
Stead, Bill, 71–73, 86
Stead Air Force Base, 73, 88
Stearman/Boeing PT-17 airplane, 205

Stearman 450 airplane, 221
Steel, Marv, 53
Stinson L-5 airplane, 221
Stock Planes, 73
Stunt pilots. See Showmanship
ST sportplanes, 205

T-6 airplane, 78
T-38 airplane, 44
Taarnhoj (pilot), 136
Tabart, Anthony, 135–36, 140
Tallman, Frank, 38–48
TBF Avenger airplane, 223
Tereshkova, Valentina, 153
Thompson Trophy Races, 68, 69, 71, 76
Tiger Moth airplane, 191–95, 200, 221
Tirpitz (battleship), 213
Torva Sprite sailplane, 132
Tracy Airport, 159
Turner, Roscoe, 68–69, 70–71, 76
Turner-Hughes, Toc H, 194
Twin Beech airplane, 47
Tyson, Geoffrey, 194

Union Switch and Signal Company, 197
United Aircraft Company, 71
U.S. Weather Bureau maps, 121
Unlimited airplanes, 73, 74, 75, 81, 83

Varkozi (pilot), 136
Viitanen (pilot), 137
VJ-23 Swingwing (hang glider), 109
Voss (pilot), 136
Vršac, Yugoslavia, soaring competition at (1972), 133–38

Waagmeester, Ron, 86
Waco airplanes, 198, 200, 202–7; model-designation system, 203–4
Waco 10 airplane, 195

Waco UPF-7 airplane, 202–7
Waco YKC Custom airplane, 46
Wagner, Arnold, 28
Waikerie, Australia, soaring competition at
   (1974), 138–42, 143
War Aircraft Replicas (WAR), 212
Warner airplanes, 198
Warplanes, 210–28
Wave soaring, 122
Wedell-Williams Meteor airplane, 69, 70–71
Wiener, E. D., 78
Wildcat airplane, 220–28
Williams, Neil, 33
Wills, Philip, 141
Wings (motion picture), 37
Wittman, Steve, 68, 71
Wittman Tailwind airplane, 169–70, 196
Wlassics, Istvan, 140

World War I, 67, 189, 194, 195
World War II, 68, 71, 78, 84; warplanes,
   210–28
Wright Brothers, 103, 109, 111

Yak 18 airplane, 28
Youngman flaps, 215

Zegels, Bert, 140
Zero airplanes, 211, 226–27
Zlin airplanes, 28, 33–36
Zlin 26 airplane, 36
Zlin 126 Trener II airplane, 36
Zlin 226 airplane, 36
Zlin 526 AFS airplane, 36
Zlin 526-L airplane, 36
Zlin Z-526 airplane, 33